"*Loveable* helped me shift from deep self-loathing to radical self-acceptance. In *The Road Less Triggered*, Dr. Kelly Flanagan goes even further—reawakening my commitment to live openhearted in a world that often teaches us to shut down. This book is practical, poetic, and deeply personal. Kelly doesn't just point to the path—he walks it and invites us to walk it too. I'll be recommending this one for years to come."

Eric Deschamps, business and leadership coach, Rhapsody Strategies; cohost, *Living Richly* podcast; creator, The Foundry

"No one names the thing beneath the thing quite like Dr. Kelly Flanagan. In *The Road Less Triggered*, he walks with us into the unseen terrains of our hearts, illuminating the hidden patterns that spark conflict and dim connection. Through his steady, peace-filled wisdom, he offers not quick fixes but practices that reshape us from the inside out. This is a book to savor, return to, and be changed by—again and again."

Ashton Gustafson, host, *Good / True / & Beautiful* podcast

"James 1:19 tells us to 'be quick to listen, slow to speak and slow to become angry.' In *The Road Less Triggered*, Dr. Flanagan gives us the path to living out this verse. This book is not another 'conflict' book. Instead, Dr. Flanagan walks with us on a path to a deeper understanding of ourselves and why we do what we do, which will result in healthier, more compassionate relationships."

Kim Kimberling, PhD, president, Awesome Marriage

"*The Road Less Triggered* is a gold mine of real-life insights and relatable examples for navigating our triggers. It's a firm, humbling reminder that while it's easy to blame the world around us, true peace comes only from looking inward."

Brian Macdonald, Judah & the Lion

"Dr. Kelly Flanagan has a gift for making the hard stuff feel doable. *The Road Less Triggered* doesn't just explain why we get stuck in the same arguments—it shows us how to pause, stay open, and choose connection when it matters most. As a dad, I know this isn't just personal growth—it's about modeling calm and compassion so our kids grow up in homes that feel safe and connected. This is a book I'll be handing to friends who want more peace and depth at home."

Jon Vroman, founder, Front Row Dads

"As a client of Kelly's, I've gained insight each time we have spoken. I thought, *What more could I possibly learn? Surely I have all of these tools?* And yet, I learned MORE goodness to add into my relationships. Specifically, I learned that I not only need to CURE my heart after it closes, I also need to feel the CARE for my heart in order for it to open back up. In a world full of quick fixes and making problems 'go away,' Kelly guides us into understanding and practicing an open heart. This tiny little tidbit is just a small piece of the bigger picture that was gleaned from *The Road Less Triggered*, yet it allowed me to communicate my needs in such a simple and understandable way."

Jamie Lee Sheils, *Wall Street Journal* bestselling author; cohost, *18 Summers Podcast for Parents*; roadschooling trophy mom of five; soulmate to a feral entrepreneur

"Reading *Man's Search for Meaning* many years ago was one of the most powerful events of my life. 'Between stimulus and response, there is a space. In that space is our power to choose our response.' This principle was etched within my soul immediately and opened new doors of possibility. Still within all its wisdom, and with all my efforts over the years, I learned it was harder to grasp and follow through on than expected, until now. For the first time, thanks to this book, I finally feel equipped to be able to put this foundational principle to work consistently and effectively in all areas of my life. Kelly has simplified the sciences around Frankl's work with step-by-step guides, along with real stories of people achieving true peace of mind, success, and the power of living with an open heart."

Jim Sheils, lucky father, husband, *Wall Street Journal* and *USA Today* bestselling author

"We know we need help. We lose our tempers. We snap at strangers and hurt the ones we love. And we keep doing the things we do not want to do. With psychological depth and soulful storytelling, Dr. Kelly Flanagan's *The Road Less Triggered* offers a path toward a gentler way of being in the world."

Katherine Willis Pershey, pastor, author of *Very Married* and *Love Letters to God*

"In *The Road Less Triggered*, Dr. Kelly shines a light on the subtle moments that derail connection. His wisdom helps us pause, stay present, and choose love over defensiveness. This book will be a game changer for your relationships."

Mike McCarthy, cofounder, Gobundance

THE ROAD LESS TRIGGERED

THE ROAD LESS

TRIGG

Books by
Dr. Kelly Flanagan

Loveable
True Companions
The Unhiding of Elijah Campbell

ERED

Turning Conflict into Connection with a Single Choice

DR. KELLY FLANAGAN

a division of Baker Publishing Group
Grand Rapids, Michigan

Published by Revell
a division of Baker Publishing Group
Grand Rapids, Michigan
RevellBooks.com

Printed in the United States of America

Library of Congress Cataloging-in-Publication Data
Names: Flanagan, Kelly PhD, author
Title: The road less triggered : turning conflict into connection with a single choice / Dr. Kelly Flanagan.
Description: Grand Rapids, Michigan : Revell, a division of Baker Publishing Group, [2026] | Includes bibliographical references.
Identifiers: LCCN 2025035052 | ISBN 9780800747558 paperback | ISBN 9780800747879 casebound | ISBN 9781493452705 ebook
Subjects: LCSH: Interpersonal communication | Interpersonal relations | Interpersonal conflict. | Conflict management.
Classification: LCC BF637.C45 F559 2026
LC record available at https://lccn.loc.gov/2025035052

The names and details of the people and situations described in this book have been changed or presented in composite form in order to ensure the privacy of those with whom the author has worked.

Cover design by Chris Kuhatschek

Illustrations by Phil Lashley

The author is represented by the literary agency of Helmers Literary Services, www.helmersliterary.com.

Baker Publishing Group publications use paper produced from sustainable forestry practices and postconsumer waste whenever possible.

26 27 28 29 30 31 32 7 6 5 4 3 2

To Donna and Gary,
whose open hearts have made so many of us
feel at home in this world

Between stimulus and response there is a space.
In that space is our power to choose our response.
In our response lies our growth and our freedom.

Viktor Frankl

Contents

It's Your Choice

> Choices are the hinges of destiny.
>
> Pythagoras

There is a moment that repeats itself over and over again in your life.

It can happen anytime and anywhere, but it occurs most commonly in your relationships. It's the moment when togetherness turns into tension, connectedness devolves into defensiveness, harmony gives way to hostility, or communication collapses into conflict. It's the last thing you want in your marriage, your parenting, your family, your friendships, or your business, but in the moment, you probably feel powerless to change it.

You know the moment all too well, yet in many ways it remains a mystery.

You catch yourself replaying the scene in your mind, searching for a solution. You resolve to do something different during it. You probably even have some success here and there, but it doesn't last. Eventually, the moment always wins, as your best intentions revert to knee-jerk reactions. Perhaps you plan to speak up, but instead you clam up. Or the opposite: You plan to calm down, but instead you throw down. Perhaps you get preachy and pedantic—a little smirky, a bit judgy, a touch controlling—and it pushes away the people you want to pull close. Before you know it, you're firing off a text or an email you'll regret tomorrow, or your date night has jumped the tracks, or the car ride with your kid has become one more brick in the wall of an increasingly alienated relationship.

Afterward, you feel defeated by the seemingly inevitable repetition of it all. Stuck in the cycle. Trapped in its triggers. The prisoner of a pattern. You might go through seasons of relative tranquility, yet, despite your best efforts, two steps forward turn into three steps back. Between episodes, you may forget about it altogether. However, in the middle of an episode, you carry the stress of it in your body throughout the day, and you may lose sleep over it at night. Your preoccupation with it disrupts your presence and diminishes your productivity. You worry you're doing irreparable harm to the most valuable assets in your life: your relationships.

You may even feel hopeless about saving them.

In an interview with author Malcolm Gladwell, relationship scientist John Gottman reported that "people are in one of two states in a relationship," and went on to describe those two states:

> The first is what I call positive sentiment override . . . where positive emotion overrides irritability. It's like a buffer. Their spouse will do something bad, and they'll say, "Oh, he's just in a crummy mood." Or they can be in negative sentiment override, so that even a relatively neutral thing that a partner says gets perceived as negative. In the negative sentiment override state, people draw lasting conclusions about each other. If their spouse does something positive, it's a selfish person doing a positive thing. It's really hard to change those states. . . . Once they start going down, toward negative emotion, ninety-four percent will continue going down.[1]

In other words, once the moment hits, 94 percent of us no longer feel free to choose connection over conflict in our most important relationships.

This book is about restoring your choice when you're triggered.

Triggered is a word our culture has taken to extremes. On the one hand, we use it in a strictly clinical way, tethering it to trauma and medical diagnoses like post-traumatic stress disorder (PTSD). In that sense, *triggered* is a word reserved for a relatively exclusive group of exceptionally wounded people. On the other hand, the word *triggered* has also been hijacked by TikTok. Someone might get served a latte with the wrong kind of cold foam at Starbucks and lament to thousands of online followers that they were "triggered" by it. In that sense, the word is rendered trite and meaningless.

In these pages, we'll take *triggered* back from the extremes. It's not something that happens only to combat veterans. Nor is it always happening to everybody all the time almost everywhere. Rather, it's something that happens regularly and repetitively in very specific moments.

And every time it happens, you have another chance to own the moment, instead of the moment owning you.

Where Communication *Really* Breaks Down

I started falling asleep with headphones on in middle school for a couple reasons. First, I'd just bought a bajillion albums from BMG—for a penny plus shipping and handling—and there weren't enough waking hours in the day to listen to them all. Also, my friend's parents were fighters.

The first time I spent the night there, all was well until we turned out the lights, and then the arguing began. I didn't say anything. Neither did he. I figured it was a fluke and forgot about it. However, the second sleepover was a replica of the first. He climbed into the top bunk, and I climbed into the bottom. He turned off the lights, and they turned on their conflict.

I thought he'd fallen asleep when, from above me, I heard a muttered, "Sorry."

"It's okay," I said, trying to ease his embarrassment.

"No, it's not," he said. "It's stupid. Every night it's the exact same fight." Bed springs creaked overhead as he rolled over. A few minutes later, some subtle snoring suggested he'd already fallen asleep.

I just lay there listening to them. My friend was right. It was basically the same argument they'd had before. A few of the details had changed, but the gist of it hadn't: If he would just say the one thing she wanted him to say, and if she would just do the one thing he wanted her to do, it would all be over. The solutions seemed so simple to me, yet every time they'd come close to one, something would go sideways, and the whole conversation would get recycled. It never got ugly, which is to say it didn't feel dangerous, it just felt *endless*.

The third time I spent the night, I packed my Walkman, headphones, and a bunch of cassette tapes. That time, when they started arguing, my friend skipped the apology and went straight to snoring, and I eavesdropped for only a few minutes. Sure enough, the script was basically the same. I fell asleep listening to "Every Rose Has Its Thorn" by Poison and wondering why a kid could see the answers more clearly than the adults.

I suppose you could say I've been a student of relationships since a dirt bike was my best way to get around.

Later in college, when I wrote my sophomore honors thesis on marital communication, I learned my friend's parents were pretty typical: Most relationship conflict feels less like D-Day and more like Groundhog Day—that movie where Bill Murray has to repeat the same twenty-four hours over and over again. After I finished the thesis, I joined a relationship research laboratory. Could showing couples a video of themselves in conflict—and giving them just two sessions of feedback about their behavior—increase the odds of their happiness over time? We proved it could.

I went on to get a PhD from Penn State University, where I studied thousands of hours of videotaped conflict while writing a dissertation on the core relationship needs that float beneath the surface of everyday conversations like who's going to pick up Billy from school or why watching Monday night football doesn't count as a date night. Then, suddenly, I was a full-time marriage therapist with a wife of my own. Naturally, with all that training in relationships, I fixed every marriage that came through my office, and my own marriage was nothing but bliss from the very beginning.

Well. Actually.

At the office, every couple's top request was better communication, but I quickly discovered that in the real world, traditional communication training wasn't very effective at improving couples' connection. The vast majority of my clients were actually good communicators already, functioning well in their vocations as doctors, attorneys, teachers, entrepreneurs, and stay-at-home parents of bustling households. In most of their life domains, they used the communication tools they already possessed with great skill. The problem wasn't a lack of tools.

The problem was, at the most important moment in their conversation, they'd close their toolbox.

Meanwhile, at home, I was replicating all the unproductive patterns I'd learned about in my studies. Perhaps the apostle Paul said it best: "For what I want to do I do not do, but what I hate I do" (Rom. 7:15). Over and over again, I'd feel disconnected but refuse to show myself. I'd hope for peace but go on the attack instead. I'd try to forgive but turn it into a fight. I had a doctorate in communication—the most well-stocked toolbox of all—and yet I, too, would close it right when I needed it most.

Finally, I gave up.

No, we didn't get divorced, nor did I have an affair. Rather, I intentionally shifted my focus from relationship transformation to self-examination. I traded out communication tools for introspection tools. In scientific terms, this was akin to a "single-case study" or an "N-of-1 trial." In spiritual terms, it's called contemplation. Whatever you want to call it, for almost twenty years now, I've studied the way **communication breaks down not *between* people but *within* people**, and I've replicated my results with countless clients. My central finding is that our communication toolbox is the key to our relational success.

And it goes by another name.

Your Communication Toolbox

I was cofacilitating a marriage retreat for an entrepreneurial group when the other facilitator asked each couple to turn their chairs so they were facing each other with knees touching and eyes locked. Then she said, "One . . . two . . . three . . . *close* your hearts to each other," and listed a bunch of reasons to go into protection mode. Next, she reversed the instructions. "One . . . two . . . three . . . *open* your hearts to each other," and listed a bunch of reasons to go into connection mode. Then she alternated those commands for a few minutes before bringing the group back together and asking what it felt like to have their hearts closed versus open. Everybody agreed: They were now aware of how different the two states felt.

"Good," she said, "but that's not actually the most important takeaway from this exercise. This is what you need to remember more than anything else." Everyone leaned in.

"You have a choice," she said.

Everyone leaned back, letting that sink in.

Maybe you need to lean back and let that sink in too: **Your communication toolbox is your heart.** When it's open, you are in connection mode, and you have access to all the communication tools you need to consistently connect with others. When it's closed, you are in protection mode, and you forfeit your access to those tools. Furthermore, you *choose* to open or close it—you just don't realize it because the moment of choice passes so quickly and unconsciously. In the heat of the moment, it *feels* like when someone does A, B, or C, your heart automatically opens; and it *feels* like when they do X, Y, or Z, your heart automatically closes. Because we've never slowed down to examine that moment, we're mostly unaware of the choice we make in the nanosecond between what is happening to us and how we react.

Let's slow down and examine it now.

When everything is going the way you want it to, the choice to be openhearted is an easy one—so easy, in fact, that it doesn't feel like a choice at all. You just open your heart to what *is*. You let it all in. You come all the way out to meet it. When your team wins the big game, it doesn't feel like you're choosing to enjoy it—it just feels like celebration. In fact, your heart is subtly opening like that all the time, and you let it.

My heart naturally opens to my first sip of coffee in the morning.

Sunrises over the Atlantic and sunsets over the Great Plains.

Good weather at my tee time and good moods at dinnertime.

A walk in the woods.

Peppermint Patties.

My wife's approval.

People doing what I believe is best for them.

God answering my prayers according to my preferences.

Did I mention my wife's approval?

Financial security.

More financial security.

Also, in case I haven't mentioned it, my wife's approval.

Our fondest memories are often formed around moments of exceptional openheartedness. When we were kids, that's what made Christmas morning so magical for so many of us—it wasn't the presents; it was that our hearts were wide open to the presents. I recall one Christmas moment in particular.

I was perhaps eight or nine years old and had fallen asleep during a ten-hour drive to spend the holiday with my beloved grandparents in the town where I'd been born. I awoke to the slowing of the car entering the city limits around midnight. The streets were empty. Christmas wreathes adorned every lamppost. Big, silent snowflakes slowly descended and zoomed toward our windshield one after the other. I was home again.

When we say something was "magical," what we really mean is it opened our heart as wide as a heart can go.

Your first sleepover with your childhood best friend. The book that made you fall in love with reading. Your first crush. The first time you tasted the freedom of driving on your own without an adult in the passenger seat pumping an imaginary brake. The first time you made art. The day you said yes to your true companion. Your firstborn in your arms. You remember each of these moments so vividly because they were moments in which you opened your heart to receive what your soul most deeply desired.

Openheartedness is what happens when you are fully experiencing the present moment without doing anything to it. When all is going well, it can feel a lot like breathing. It just happens.

It isn't until something knocks the wind out of you that you have to be intentional about getting your breath back.

Your friends have coffee without you and post it on social media. Your parents act like your parents. Your spouse does that thing that has become more and more irritating over the years. Your baby—now a teenager—makes a terrible decision that could impact the rest of their life and then acts like you're the most ignorant thing on two feet for questioning it. Someone steals your parking spot. You do your best, and someone says it's not good enough. You disclose something near and dear to your heart, and you're met with a blank stare. You ask for love but all you get is lip service. You send a thoughtful text and never hear back. You feel lonely, ashamed, wronged, rejected, misjudged, abandoned, threatened, overwhelmed, scared, panicked, intimidated, lost, frustrated, or enraged. The list goes on and on. However, this isn't a book about *what* knocks the wind out of us.

It's a book about what to *do* when the wind gets knocked out of us.

It's a book about the split-second decision you make when you're triggered and your heart reflexively closes to what's happening: *Will you let it close, or will you keep it open?* In other words, it's about the practice of openheartedness, which is the conscious choice to fully experience the present moment as it is, especially when it's not going the way you want it to. It's about how to handle any moment that is breaking badly so you can show up to that moment with your best stuff.

I flew home from that couples' retreat finally knowing what to call the communication toolbox and knowing I had a choice to keep it open or not. Then, for eighteen of the most painful months of my life, I completely ignored the choice.

Three Big Questions

On December 31, 2020, I was broken. Literally. The year had laid me low.

It began in January, when my best friend and I dissolved our business partnership *and* our friendship. Inside, my heart was breaking, but on the outside, I'm guessing my closed heart looked cold and calculating. Two months later, COVID-19 hit. My wife and I were faced with the unprecedented challenge of transforming our in-person therapy practices into online businesses. Meanwhile, the kids were schooling at home and quickly becoming Zoombies. My heart was closed to all of it. One afternoon, I decided to blow off steam on a bike ride—a dangerous mindset for high-speed cycling. Just moments into an incautious ride, I flew over the handlebars and shattered my left collarbone on an asphalt road.

They say that bones heal stronger in the broken places. Mine didn't. "Fibrous tissue non-union fractures," they called them. Basically, I now have two hinges in that collarbone where before there were none.

The nature of the injury meant a lengthy rehabilitation, so by the end of the year my body was out of shape, and on New Year's Eve I found myself contemplating fitness resolutions for the coming year. Keto vs. paleo. Intermittent fasting versus 5:2. Cardio versus strength training. It was just then, while searching the internet for fitness plans, that I came across this quote: "Do not let anything that happens in life be important enough that you're willing to close your heart over it."[2]

It was a wake-up call: My spiritual heart was in even worse shape than my physical one. It was almost always closed, and even when it was open, it would close again on a hair trigger. A change in my physical condition would need to begin with a change to my emotional condition. Right then and there, I made my New Year's resolution:

Moment to moment, I will notice my heart closing and try to open it back up.

Most New Year's resolutions are abandoned by the third week of January. Not this one. Years later, openheartedness has become my core life practice. It is my most sacred spiritual discipline. The apostle Paul exhorted us to pray without ceasing. The practice of openheartedness is my prayer, and every day the choice gets clearer and quicker. So why did I wait so long to start making the choice?

Because I had the same three questions about it that everyone does.

— — —

Can I be openhearted and have boundaries at the same time?

After delivering a keynote to a group of hard-charging entrepreneurial women in Costa Rica, the first question from the audience was, "I want to be openhearted toward my employees, but it wouldn't be appropriate to tell them everything about my personal life, would it?" When openheartedness is initially suggested to someone with more "doing" energy, the first question on their mind is usually, "Oh no, how much am I going to have to divulge?" They worry about how much they will have to *reveal*. They fear a lack of boundaries about what will come *out* of them.

In contrast, after introducing openheartedness to my online community, several of them feared it would turn them into doormats. "I'm just learning to have boundaries with people," one person said, "and it sounds like I'd have to let them walk all over me again." When openheartedness is initially suggested to someone with more "being" energy, the first question on their mind is usually, "Oh no, how much am I going to have to take?" They worry about how much they will have to *receive*. They fear a lack of boundaries about what will get *into* them.

Both reactions represent a common misconception about the relationship between the inner condition of our heart and the outer action of our boundary setting. What these reactions reveal is that we've gotten into the bad habit of using a closed heart to set our boundaries. The truth is, **an open heart doesn't make your boundaries weaker, it makes your boundaries wiser.** Every time you hold your heart open intentionally while holding your boundaries consciously, you are being transformed into a healthier and holier human being. You've learned how to have limits and how to love at the same time.

If it feels like openhearted boundary setting is a big iceberg and we're only addressing the tip of it here, you're right. In chapter 7, we'll explore the whole iceberg.

— — —

Why would I want to open my heart to hard things?

"I try to stay positive," a client says to me. "I mean, if something tragic happens, I'll feel it with the best of them, but otherwise I don't really see the point of dwelling on things." Meanwhile, on the split screen, tears streak his wife's cheeks beneath red-rimmed eyes. She's just had a biopsy and is waiting for the results. "Why would I open up to her negativity when we don't know anything definitive yet?" he asks.

I tell him about the Fox River that runs through northern Illinois. The Army Corps of Engineers recently recommended the removal of several human-made dams along the river, because any benefit of the dams is far outweighed by the ecological damage caused by shallow waters downriver. Our experiences are like that river, I tell him; when we close our heart to experiences that are meant to move through us, we create more problems downriver than we solve. Then I share some ancient Eastern wisdom.

"Pain is inevitable, suffering is optional," I say.

Therapist and bestselling author Lori Gottlieb puts it this way: "There's a difference between pain and suffering. . . . You're going to have to feel pain—everyone feels pain at times—but you don't have to suffer so much. You're not choosing the pain, but you're choosing the suffering."[3] In other words, if you open your heart to something hard, you'll feel the pain briefly, but then it will pass. However, if you close your heart to it, you now have the pain still waiting to be experienced, as well as the suffering created by your closing.

"The pain right now," I say, "is your wife's sadness, while the unnecessary suffering created by your closed heart is the disconnection between the two of you in the midst of it, and the conflict that will come from that disconnection."

The forms of unnecessary suffering downriver from a closed heart are countless. We've already covered many of them. Conflict and coldness. Division and divorce. There are also compulsively avoidant and sometimes addictive behaviors. For example, when you want to close your heart to what's happening in your life, scrolling, browsing, working, drinking, and using drugs all make effective dams, for a while. They can also make for tremendous suffering downriver. Furthermore, when you block pain, you also have to block pleasure. **Joy and sorrow are not separate rivers—when you open your heart, they flow as one.** If we dam up sorrow, we dam up joy. Then we wonder why it feels so stagnant and lifeless downriver.

As you close your heart to difficult things, your life gets smaller and smaller, one choice at a time.

Okay, but how do you open your heart?

In the early days of 2021, following the resolution to open my heart whenever it closed, that was the question I most needed to answer. I traced the quote that had inspired my resolution to a book, but it was light on instruction. To open your heart, the author suggested, you simply "relax and release."[4] Easier said than done.

Over the next several years, I drew upon my decades of psychological training in communication and relationships, a range of scientific disciplines beyond my own, the core tenets of the world's faith and wisdom traditions, and plenty of trial-and-error learning to hone the process by which anyone can restore their freedom to stay openhearted and to cultivate calm connection, even in their most triggered moments. I call it the Peaceful Pivot Process.

In these pages, it will take you only a few hours of reading to learn what it took me years to discover.

Peaceful Pivot Process

The structure of this book mirrors the process I've developed for teaching people how to live openheartedly. It happens in three parts, with three steps in each part.

Part I: Get Calm. In chapter 1, you'll learn to see conflict coming significantly sooner by tapping into your underutilized sixth sense and turning your bodily sensations into early warning signs of the coming closure. This is an essential foundation of openheartedness, because the earlier you can observe your heart close, the more easily you can keep your heart open. In chapter 2, you'll learn why you can't defeat your defensiveness, but how you can delay it long enough to disrupt it. In doing so, you'll begin to wedge that nanosecond of choice apart just a little more. In chapter 3, you'll utilize that extra space to cultivate calmness before connectedness. As you make tending to your triggered nervous system your top priority, you'll experience a rapid decrease in the dysfunction caused by dysregulation.

At that point, you may be tempted to stop there, because it will kinda-sorta feel like it's working.

There'll be fewer fights and a little more connection, and you'll feel a bit more relaxed. However, you'll periodically find yourself triggered and right back at square one, revealing how much you're still just white-knuckling this openheartedness thing. White-knuckling isn't very much fun. It's not freedom. It's a daily pop quiz, and you pass it more than you used to, but you're still getting a B- in the class. I'd encourage you to skip this interlude and go right into part two.

Part II: Get Free. In chapter 4, we'll explore the possibility that it's not the people *around* you who are triggering your heart to close but an experience *within* you. Here, we'll simplify the solution to all your triggered moments by identifying the source of them within you. In chapter 5, you'll turn your triggered moments into a time machine, tracing them throughout your story, helping you understand how the past is unconsciously driving your reactions in the present. In chapter 6, you'll feel your way to freedom by allowing the pain of your past to flow rather than fester.

This part concludes with a deep sense of inner safety. As you begin to feel genuinely comfortable in your own skin—even during your most triggered moments—you'll be tasting some true freedom for the first time, and you may be tempted to enter a second kind of interlude, in which you bypass potential conflict completely. You'll feel your heart closing and have the power to simply walk away with an open heart. However, this will eventually reveal itself to be just as unsatisfying as the closing. **We're not here to walk away, we're here to walk together.**

I'd encourage you to skip this interlude as well and jump right into part three.

Part III: Get Connected. In chapter 7, we'll take everything you've learned previously and put it to work for you and your relationships by showing you how to set sincere boundaries without battles. Specifically, we'll explore a third way beyond the boundarylessness of codependence and the harsh boundaries of independence. You'll learn a method for setting healthy, openhearted, *interdependent* boundaries.

The establishment of true interdependence often represents a sort of golden age of openheartedness for many people, but, like any golden age, it can't last forever. There will be "failures" of openheartedness. By the time you're through with chapter 8, though, you'll realize there is no such thing as a failure. By harnessing your newfound power to remain curious, each new closing will be transformed into an opportunity for even deeper connection with yourself and your people.

Finally, in chapter 9, you'll begin to experience the mastery that comes when someone closes their heart to you and you instantly perceive the pain beneath their protection. This kind of compassion is the pinnacle of openhearted connection, and it can be practiced in the bedroom and the boardroom and every space in between, transforming each of those spaces into a place of peaceful connection.

It's a way of being truly together without interlude.

The Freedom to Turn Both Ways

When I was a boy—in the years before headphones helped me fall asleep—I lived in a trailer park, my clothes came from rummage sales, and the kitchen cupboards were stocked with Kraft Macaroni & Cheese.

Also, my mode of transportation was a car that couldn't turn left.

It was a gold, decades-old Buick Skylark. End-to-end, it couldn't have been much shorter than the mobile home. Its vast bench seats were upholstered in leather that smelled like dust and burned the bottoms of your legs in the summer heat. If it had seat belts, I didn't use them. And for some reason, which I never thought to question as a kid, the glittering behemoth could only make right turns. If you arrived at a four-way intersection and needed to turn left, you drove straight for a block, made three right turns to circle back to the same intersection, which you'd go straight through, and—voilà—you were back on course.

When we're triggered, we're like that old Buick Skylark—we can only turn in one direction, and usually that direction is conflict. Then, it takes many turns to get our connection back on course. Those many turns take time and fuel, and they are a wildly inefficient way to be driving through our relationships. This book is going to put you in a brand-new automobile that can turn either way at the most important intersections in your life. You'll be free to choose calm connection where before you could only turn toward conflict.

You'll be empowered, finally, to take the road less triggered.

PART I

GET CALM

> The real labor of liberation is acknowledging that there is always a choice, even though I must work to get back to that choice.
>
> Lama Rod Owens

1

Sense Conflict Coming

> It is amazing how many hints and guides and intuitions for living come to the sensitive person who has ears to hear what [their] body is saying.
>
> Rollo May

James Yingling III dedicated his life to cars, and it was ultimately a car that took his life.[1]

James owned and operated a car lot in Bedford County, Pennsylvania, where he was known to be a talented mechanic who could fix pretty much anything with an engine. On a November morning in 2013, he got into his 2006 Saturn Ion for his short commute to work. Along the route was a T-intersection he'd navigated thousands of times before. On that morning, though, instead of driving through the intersection, he crashed through it and into the ditch on the other side of the road. Even worse, the airbags didn't deploy, resulting in severe head trauma. He was flown to a nearby hospital, but by the time he arrived, he was in a coma, from which he never awoke. Two weeks later, on December 8, he was gone.

The accident report showed the car never slowed down, which could suggest suicide. However, the report also showed he was wearing a seat belt, which suggested the opposite. It seemed his loved ones would be left with the painful mystery of that morning forever.

Forever lasted less than two months.

On February 6, 2014, General Motors quietly issued a recall for a wide range of its cars of various makes and models—including the 2006 Saturn Ion—citing a faulty ignition switch. James's widow, Nadia, saw the recall notice and called a Pittsburgh attorney, who traced the totaled car to a nearby junkyard. The lawyers weren't interested in the ignition switch, though. They were looking for a special device located beneath the driver's seat.

The car's black box.

Black box is a commonly used term that originally referred to flight recorders that first appeared in military planes in World War II and collected key information about the performance of both pilot and aircraft. At the time, they were painted black, but these days they're painted orange, and they're a standard feature on most airplanes. In the early 2000s, a similar kind of instrument began appearing in automobiles. In cars, they're technically called *event data recorders* and kept in a stainless steel case, but most people still call them black boxes.

A car's black box has a very specific purpose. It doesn't record any information about conditions outside the vehicle, like weather or road conditions or the actions of other drivers. And it doesn't record comprehensive information about the vehicle's entire trip. Rather, it only records and retains data about what's happening within the car in the few seconds before and after a crash. The key data points are speed, steering, brake usage, seat belt usage, airbag functioning, and something called "throttle position"—basically, how much the engine is revving.

When the lawyers downloaded the data from the Saturn's black box, it showed two things they already knew: James never decreased his speed, and the airbags didn't deploy.[2] Disturbingly, it also showed he never turned the wheel, nor were the brakes ever engaged. However, one additional piece of data revealed the reason for his inaction: When the car crashed, the engine's rpms were at zero. The engine wasn't running. A faulty ignition switch had indeed triggered the car to turn off at random, and a car that is off can't be steered, can't be braked, and the airbags don't deploy.

At the time of the crash, the car had been utterly out of James's otherwise expert control.

This data became part of a bellwether case in a landslide of lawsuits against General Motors, who eventually had to pay damages for 124 deaths and 275 injuries related to the faulty ignition switch.[3] Furthermore, GM paid nearly a billion dollars in criminal fines to the federal government for having covered up their knowledge of the problem for more than a decade. All because one black box recorded only the data necessary to explain the crash. No more, no less.

What if you became the black box in your relationships? What if, in the few seconds before your connection crashes, you recorded only the data necessary to see your conflict coming and to steer clear of it? No more, no less.

You see, in our desire to take our relationships to the next level, we think we have to gather insights about the whole journey in order to understand its critical moments. We buy shelves of books and listen to countless podcasts. We show up to therapists with a laundry list of complaints and we spend years ticking through the list, trying to solve each of the problems one by one. Sometimes these efforts yield important insights, but the list of problems often repopulates itself, and we self-improvers become Sisyphus—pushing a rock uphill only to watch it roll down again.

What if we're all collecting way too much data about our relationships? What if, when it comes to conflict, the few seconds before and after connection crashes provide all the data we need for understanding how it happened—and how to avoid it next time?

Furthermore, in the heat of the moment, we tend to record exactly the wrong data about the crash. Unlike a black box, which records only onboard data, we tend to focus far more on what's going on outside of us rather than inside of us. For instance, we record data about the behavior of other "drivers"—what they did to trigger us—while neglecting the data about what's happening "onboard" in our body. Or we chalk it up to bad weather and slick roads—the markets are down, it's an election year, the holidays are stressful—so we don't examine it at all, and then we're caught off guard when it happens again on a perfectly sunny day. But what if the moment our heart closes—like an ignition switch suddenly turning off—is the singular reason we struggle to make it through our relational intersections safely, yet we're so busy looking out the window we fail to understand it?

The wrong data always yields the wrong answers, no matter how much of it you have.

Therefore, it's essential to understand why we collect exactly the wrong data about our conflict. It has to do with our senses. We have six, but we were only told about five of them.

Our First Five Senses: Too Little, Too Late

In kindergarten, we sat cross-legged on the classroom rug, fidgeting and wishing for recess, while our teachers taught us that we had five senses—sight, hearing, touch, taste, and smell. These five senses help us experience and understand the world around us. In that way, they are the opposite of a black box: They record data only about what is happening outside us, and they neglect to notice anything happening "onboard." That's why scientists describe them as exteroceptive senses. *Extero* means "external."

What they don't tell you in kindergarten is that your exteroceptive senses provide your brain with more data than it can handle, so it picks and chooses which sensations from the outside world it will prioritize. Not until an introductory psychology course in college do you learn about the way the brain accomplishes this sorting. It's called habituation.

For example, when you put on your clothes this morning, at first you felt the sensation of the fabric on your skin. You had thoughts like, *Ooh, this hoodie is so cozy*, or *These jeans are getting a little tight; no more dessert for me this week*. Within minutes, however, you ceased to notice those sensations. Why? Your brain determined the sensation of your clothing was both harmless and constant, so it switched its data-processing power to more important information in the outside world, like whether or not your boss is in a bad mood again or why your teenager's eyes are suspiciously bloodshot.

That's habituation, and each one of your five senses is prone to it.

Your last sip of coffee in the morning will never taste as good as your first. The hum of traffic from the interstate a mile away will fade into the background. Ten minutes after lighting a lavender candle in the living room, you won't be able to smell it anymore—yet walk out of the room for a few minutes, and upon your return you'll be hit with a wall of aroma. Last week, I drove down a street in my hometown where I've lived for the majority of my life and I saw a park I swear was never there before. In fact, it has been so consistently and harmlessly there that my mind began overlooking it.

Conflict, on the other hand, never fails to get our attention because the brain experiences it as potentially harmful, so it immediately tunes in to the sights and sounds of discord. In this way, too, your first five senses are the opposite of a black box, which records data not just during a crash but right before it as well. In contrast, your first five senses are more like a properly functioning airbag—they don't deploy until your heart is already closed and your conflict is already escalating enough to notice it happening "out there."

The first and only time I laid a hand on one of my kids, my first five senses didn't kick in until I saw the look in my oldest son's eyes. Aidan was thirteen or fourteen years old. It was late in the evening, and I was ready for bed. He was in our bedroom asking permission to do something the next day. His life philosophy has always been if you can keep them talking, there's a chance you might change their mind. He has a way with words.

I can't remember how many times I told him the conversation was over for the night, nor how many times I asked him to leave the room. After all, at that point it was still just a harmless interaction—I was habituated to it, so I wasn't recording any data. I can't even remember putting my hand on his chest and pushing him backward through the doorway. Certainly my heart was already closed by that point. When had it closed? I'll never know, because that's onboard data, and our exteroceptive senses don't store that information.

I didn't start recording data until I saw the gut-wrenching mixture of sadness and anger in his watery eyes. By getting physical, I'd broken the unspoken contract that keeps any relationship basically safe. It took a long time for our relationship to recover from that moment.

When our hearts close unconsciously, our relationships rupture unnecessarily.

Fortunately, human beings come equipped with an underutilized superpower that can quickly and immediately expand our awareness around this moment of closing, restoring to us some freedom of choice about whether we will close our heart or not. We use it all the time, but we don't know it, and so we rarely draw on it consciously. It's our *sixth* sense. It's called interoception.

And it's your black box.

Become the Black Box

Every year, our family drives from Illinois to Delaware for our annual summer beach vacation, and every summer, somewhere along the route, one of the kids announces they have to go to the bathroom. Unfortunately for them, when I plug our destination into the GPS and the app says it will take less than fourteen hours to travel nine hundred miles, I expect it to take less than fourteen hours—as if gas stops and road construction delays and bathroom breaks don't take time too. So, when they say they've got to pee, I ask them how long they can wait.

They use interoception to determine their answer.

You can try it right now. How badly do you have to go to the bathroom at this moment, on a scale from one to ten? Go ahead, I'll give you a second. Got your number? Great.

Did you notice what happened?

Your awareness, which usually resides somewhere up in your head, behind your eyes, traveled down through your body, checked on the condition of your bladder, noticed how full it felt, and then came back to report its finding. That is your sixth sense at work. It's the same sense you'd use if I asked how anxious or tired or hungry you are right now. You'd check inside your body for indicators of these conditions.

That's interoception.

Scientist Jennifer Murphy of the Royal Holloway University of London describes interoception as "the processing of bodily signals that come from the inside," while pointing out the contrast with our first five senses: "We can gauge whether we're breathless by the sound of our breath, but that's an exteroceptive, rather than an interoceptive, route to perceiving that."[4]

Sahib Khalsa, an interoception researcher at the Laureate Institute for Brain Research in Tulsa, Oklahoma, has this to say about interoception: "We know next to nothing about what's happening on the floor of the ocean. Yet we know that it's fundamentally important to determining our climate. It's the same thing with interoception. We know so little about what's happening inside of our bodies in relation to how we feel, yet we know that it's important. It cannot be ignored."[5]

Here at the beginning of the Peaceful Pivot Process, we stop ignoring the closing of our heart by tapping into our interoceptive powers. We become the black box—the event data recorder—for the moments just before our heart closes and our connection crashes. Sometimes, the information you gather can be used immediately to keep your heart open in the moment. Sometimes, your heart closes anyway, and the information becomes an invaluable resource for noticing your closing even earlier next time, which will restore even more of your freedom to choose.

As you practice conscious interoception—and your awareness of your closing expands—you'll become more and more sensitive to its earliest warning signs. More specifically, you'll notice an uncomfortable sensation somewhere between your waist and your temples. No human being has ever said, "I felt my heart close, and my toes cramped." Waist to temples. That's where it's at.

In your gut, a clenching or wrenching or the merest of butterflies or that little pit in the center of your stomach. In your lower back, an ache or a twitch or a spasm. In your lower sternum, a thickening or tightening, a fullness, a turning inward on itself. The chest is where a closing heart most commonly manifests in the body. For instance, when the closing of my heart is fast and furious, it feels like two big, thick stainless steel security doors slamming closed—one coming from my left armpit, one coming from my right, meeting in the middle of my anxiety-filled chest. People often describe something burning like a white-hot sun in the middle of their solar plexus. Or something heavy, like a big black hole. Maybe for you it manifests higher up—that knot between your shoulder blades your massage therapist can never get out. Perhaps a constricting of your airway or the proverbial lump in your throat. A pressure behind your eyes that never condenses into tears. Throbbing at your temples. Lightheadedness. Seeing red.

"Experiencing the sensations of our minds and bodies reduces reactivity and allows us to experience fluidity," writes Lama Rod Owens. "When there is more fluidity, there is more potential for care, and that care helps us to reduce violence against ourselves and others."[6]

When it comes to a closing heart, your body is like Paul Revere riding through the night—an advanced messenger sending notice of the coming conflagration. If you can use your interoception to become aware of these sensations as soon as they begin, you will have tuned in to the most important moment in your relationships while you still have the freedom to respond rather than react.

And your Paul Reverian interoception can give you far more warning than you might imagine.

Had you been living in Iowa City in the 1990s, you might have responded to an advertisement recruiting participants for a curious experiment on decision-making.[7] It involved four decks of cards with monetary rewards and penalties on their undersides, a sum of money to gamble with, and a galvanic skin response (GSR) sensor attached to your palm to measure your arousal. The assigned task was to flip cards so that over the course of the experiment you would earn more money than you lost.

What the researchers didn't tell you is that the decks were stacked. The two bad decks had cards with high rewards but even higher penalties, so if you flipped only those cards, you'd be certain to end up in debt. In contrast, the two good decks contained cards with low rewards but even lower penalties, so if you flipped only those cards you'd be guaranteed to end up with a profit. They also didn't tell you that they weren't really interested in the money. They were actually studying how long it took people to realize—both consciously and unconsciously—that the bad decks were dangerous.

This is what they found:

If you were the typical participant, it took you approximately fifty flips to express a conscious hunch the bad decks were dangerous, and another thirty flips to conclude for certain that you were done flipping them. However, something else was happening outside of your awareness. Way back at the tenth card flip—right around the time the researchers noticed you began choosing the bad decks less frequently—the GSR sensor revealed that your palms started sweating. Ten cards versus fifty cards. In other words, you interoceptively registered the danger of the bad decks *80 percent* sooner than your exteroceptive senses allowed, but it was unconscious, so you couldn't fully utilize the data. In the Iowa laboratory, conscious interoception would have produced more profits.

In the real world, conscious interoception will produce more peace.

Imagine what you could do with 80 percent more warning that your heart is closing to your people like they're a bad deck of cards and you're about to choose conflict over connection. It could make the difference—at the most important intersections in your relationships—between your connection crashing helplessly into a fatal crisis versus navigating smoothly through the twists and turns of love and life.

Become the black box. **Don't pay attention to what's happening around you, pay attention to what's tightening within you.** Turn your interoception into an event data recorder. Feel it in your body first. Tune in to what it's telling you right now about what your heart is going to do very soon, rather than waiting for the wreckage to show you what has already happened.

If you do so, you will have already harnessed some of your power to peacefully pivot and to keep your heart open.

Exercise: Name Your Number

I admit two people to my Zoom room for a first coaching appointment. We'll call them Henry and Sarah Hill, and we'll be following their progress through the Peaceful Pivot Process for the rest of this book.

Henry appears first. His receding hairline is styled immaculately. Permanent creases between his eyebrows suggest those eyebrows are furrowed on a regular basis. A virtual background is emblazoned with his company logo—a mountain, one side of it a jagged blue arrow pointing toward the peak, with "Hilltop Investments" written into the mountainside itself.

Sarah appears next. Her hair is pulled back tightly into a high pony. She's either a cosmetics master or she's not wearing any makeup. Some sunspots here and there suggest the latter and are the only sign she's in her thirties. Her background is not virtual—tall white kitchen cabinets partially obscure a living room with a large television above the fireplace and toys littering the floor.

We do the can-you-hear-me-can-you-see-me thing before I say how much I've been looking forward to this first appointment. My enthusiasm is not reciprocated. Henry's jaw is clenched and undulating at the joint. Sarah's eyes are vacant, her lips a thin straight line.

"Well," I say, "it doesn't take a rocket scientist to see I'm interrupting something."

Humor as litmus test. They just stare at the screen. It must be a whopper. *Good*, I think. *Why waste time?*

"I'll begin many of our appointments with an exercise I call Name Your Number. Basically, you'll quantify the state of your heart on a scale from one to ten, with one being as closed-hearted as can be, like you don't want to be here and you're not even sure if you want to be with this person, and ten being as openhearted as can be, like the day you fell in love or the day you decided to get married. So, what is the state of your heart in this moment?"

I wait as they engage in a Zoom stare-off, neither one wanting to open up enough to go first.

Finally, Henry breaks the silence.

"I don't understand the metric," he says. "It seems subjective."

"Good point," I say. "To start, imagine yourself at a one. What does it feel like in your body at those times? Now, imagine yourself at a ten. How differently does your body feel at those moments? I'm going to give you something called the See It Sooner Self-Inventory* to help you fine-tune these observations. Over time, you'll become so skilled at this you'll know exactly the thoughts, feelings, and bodily sensations that go along with a three versus a seven, for instance. Also, keep in mind, naming your number aloud is not about being right, per se, but about being just a little more open. Once you own your closing, your closing no longer owns you."

Henry sighs. "I guess I'm about a two. I could close a little more, but not much."

Sarah quickly follows. "I'm a four."

"Good job," I say. "And I bet after saying it out loud, you feel like about a two-and-a-half and a four-and-a-half?"

The vacant looks on their faces suggest they're using their interoception to go inward and check.

"Huh," says Henry, "yeah, it feels a little better."

"Me too," confirms Sarah.

*For a free download of resources like the See It Sooner Self-Inventory, see the "Take Action" sections of the Discussion Guide at the end of this book.

I smile. "Imagine if you can move that awareness all the way forward to the moment in which you first begin to close. You'll increase your power to stay open and bypass much of the relationship rupture and repair you've been spending so much of your time and energy on." Sarah's eyes are more alive again. Henry is leaning in.

"So how do we move that awareness forward?" he asks.

I suggest they take me back to the beginning of this particular conflict, and we'll see what we notice.

Sarah, now more openhearted, forgets her vow to never go first. "We had a really good week together, so we decided to have friends over to watch March Madness last night. They have kids who are seven and four, about Owen's and Grace's ages, so the kids all get along and can sort of babysit each other, and we really like hanging out with Doug and Amber. They stayed way after the games were over, so we got the kids to bed late and didn't have time to clean up."

I interrupt again. "What were your numbers when you went to sleep?"

"I was a ten," Henry says without hesitation. "It was a great night."

"Nine," adds Sarah.

"Okay, go on," I say to her.

"Well, this morning the kids were crabby, and the house looked like a hurricane hit it. I'm supposed to get us packed for spring break today, and I could tell I wasn't going to get it done. I could just imagine Henry's reaction when he gets home and the suitcases aren't at the back door. Meanwhile, he's getting himself ready for his day like he doesn't have a care in the world. So I told him I wished I could count on him to help with things, and he just exploded."

"Number at that point?" I ask.

"Six," she says.

"Henry?"

Henry's jaw is visibly tightening as he speaks through it. "I was probably a five at that point, but I didn't explode. I raised my voice. And listen, I'd been feeling great. We'd had the best week we've had in a while and a great time with friends. I just wanted to enjoy that for a while longer, and here comes Sarah, focused on everything that is wrong, criticizing me for not doing more. We could have had a great family breakfast. A ten, you know? But she made it impossible."

They both look at me as if to say, *Can you please fix my spouse?*

"This is all still so fresh," I say, "so it's a great opportunity to see even earlier into the closing of your hearts. Henry, let's start with you. When and where did you first feel it in your body?"

"I mean, obviously, I felt angry when she criticized me."

"And where did you feel that in your body?"

He pauses for a moment—travels through time with his memory and through his body with his interoception—before returning. "In my stomach." He pats a spot on his body off camera.

"And what did it feel like there?"

"It felt like a clenching. But hot. Like a ball of fire growing fast." He pauses. "Then I felt it in my head. I just saw red. Honestly, given what I was feeling, I think I did a pretty good job not flying totally off the handle."

"I'd like to challenge you a little more there," I say. "This isn't your and Sarah's first rodeo. I'm guessing there was a part of you that might have even expected her reaction to that kind of morning. Do you recall anything even sooner?"

He sits back, still, then his shoulders slump in the universal sign of a blind spot being seen. "Yeah," he says. "Now that you mention it. Right after we woke up, we were at our sinks, brushing our teeth, and she said something about how much she had to do today. It triggered me a little bit."

"In what way?"

"I felt some tightness in my chest. I guess you could call it anxiety." A wry smile appears on his face. "That's actually why

I was acting so chipper. I wanted to keep the positive vibe from last week going, and I could tell she was going to the dark side."

"The dark side," I repeat. "That's a powerful phrase. No wonder you felt anxious."

Sarah has been listening patiently, but her patience is gone. "It's not my dark side," she protests. "It's my realistic side. It's my not-a-robot side. It's being overwhelmed and wanting to not feel so alone in it. What's so bad about that?"

"Sarah," I ask, "when did you first notice your heart closing?"

"When he blew up," she replies instantly. "It's like a veil dropped over my whole head." She waves both hands around her hair. "It's a foggy feeling. It's just way easier to stay inside here than to fight a losing battle."

"I'm going to challenge you too. You mentioned that before you asked Henry for help, you were already imagining him disappointed with you." Instantly, her eyes grow wet and red-rimmed.

"Yes," she admits. "I pictured him walking in the door all excited and asking how the packing went, and I got anxious."

"Anxious, not angry? Why do you say anxious? How did you feel it in your body?"

She uses her own memory and interoception. "It was the butterfly feeling in my stomach. Maybe a little panic in my chest."

By the end of the hour, Henry and Sarah will be aware that their closings actually began the night before. When Henry looked around the messy house, he predicted Sarah's stress in the morning and was already closing to her "dark side." Sarah had lain in bed for an hour before falling asleep, trying to figure out how she'd get it all done on her own and how she might ask Henry for help without triggering his anger. Earlier in the hour, they'd named their numbers at bedtime as a ten and a nine. By the end of the hour, Henry realized his had actually been an eight and Sarah identified hers had been a seven. Progress.

They're learning to sense their conflict coming.

2

Disrupt Your Defensiveness

> The situation is difficult, and many people say, "Don't just sit there, do something." But doing more things may make the situation worse. So you should say, "Don't just do something, sit there." Sit there, stop, be yourself first, and begin from there.
>
> Thich Nhat Hanh

Will Smith was the Waldo of my formative years—he showed up on every page.

When he was still the Fresh Prince, "Parents Just Don't Understand" was a middle school anthem of mine, and I never missed an episode of *The Fresh Prince of Bel-Air*. The song "Summertime" has been a staple on my seasonal playlist since the day it was released. In my college dorm room, I hung a poster of an iconic image from *Independence Day*—Will chomping a cigar after knocking an alien out with a right hook. When I met my wife, "Gettin' Jiggy Wit It" was a radio hit, and we could both do the dance.

So, on the afternoon of March 27, 2022, with the Oscars just hours away, and Will the favorite to win Best Actor for his performance in *King Richard*, I was racing through the final pages of his memoir. It seemed fitting to finish his story about scaling the mountain of stardom on the day he reached the summit. The book had already spent seventeen weeks on *The New York Times* bestseller list, won the NAACP Image Award for Outstanding Literary Achievement, and Oprah had called it the best memoir of all time.

I was in agreement with her, until the last three chapters.

Will described a conflict with his wife, Jada, that brought their relationship to the breaking point and launched them each on journeys of personal healing. Will started by retreating to a friend's home in the Caribbean, where he encountered his inability to be still. So he followed that experience with a two-week silent retreat at his property in the mountains of Utah, which initiated a binge of spiritual literature.

I added several of the titles he cited to my own stack.

After the retreat, he began several years of psychotherapy. During the work, he discovered two defenses that had protected him since he was a kid. He called his "nice-guy" defense Uncle Fluffy—a "strategic childhood persona" he'd crafted to entertain people and endear them to him so they would never turn against him.[1] He also identified Fluffy's counterpart, who he called the General. When Fluffy failed, it was the General's job to strong-arm his way to approval and to punish those who didn't get on board. "These personas weave a universe in which you are trapped," his therapist explained to him.[2]

At that point I was still nodding along, recalling when I first experienced my own closed-hearted defensiveness as more prison than protection.

Will's answer to his entrapment was to participate in a psychedelic ayahuasca ceremony in the Amazon jungle, during which he had a transcendent experience of his own inner beauty.

He described it as the "unparalleled greatest feeling [he'd] ever had."[3] He would go on to do thirteen more psychedelic ceremonies. That's when some uneasiness set in for me. *Fourteen* ceremonies. It seemed like someone chasing a new high, not healing an old wound.

Then, in the final pages of the memoir, Will described bungee jumping into the Grand Canyon, suggesting he'd overcome his childhood trauma and all the fear it inspired, even the fear of death. His heart was wide open and, he seemed to be saying, it would never close again. When I closed the book, though, my uneasiness was in full bloom.

"So," my wife asked, "what did you think of it?"

"It was great until the ending. Will thinks he's conquered his defenses." I knew that was impossible; just when you think a defense has been vanquished, it comes back with a vengeance.

A few hours later, the Oscars emcee Chris Rock made a joke about Jada that replicated Will's childhood wounds about a man (his father) hurting the woman he loved (his mother). Uncle Fluffy showed up first, initially laughing along with the joke. But Fluffy was quickly replaced by the General, who walked up onstage and hit Chris Rock with a slap heard 'round the world. I was shocked but not surprised. Will had indeed learned—in the most public classroom of all time, with twelve million people watching—a lesson we must all ultimately learn in the Peaceful Pivot Process:

You don't defeat your defensiveness by doing *away* with it, you defeat your defensiveness by doing *nothing* with it.

Will's mistake was a common one: As we become aware of *when* our heart closes, most of us will want to eliminate *how* our heart closes. This is a totally natural instinct. Having become all too aware of the unnecessary wreckage caused by our closing, it makes sense we'd want to prevent the whole thing from happening. Now that we can see our window of choice, which of us wouldn't want to cancel our closing?

Countless gurus throughout the ages have tried to sell the kind of finish line where you've outraced your defensiveness and left it in the dust. Sadly, their students almost always end up like Will, albeit usually with a smaller audience watching. The defenses you've come to depend upon can't be dismissed, discarded, or destroyed. They can't be fixed, healed, or transformed. Your heart will forever be triggered to close. Your defenses will always be standing at the ready, waiting to come to your aid. You don't pivot by becoming defenseless; you pivot by surrendering to the presence of your defenses and softening to their purpose.

When you can welcome what's inside of you forever, you can work with what comes out of you today.

The Anatomy of Our Defensiveness

The science of acute stress has been telling us for over a hundred years that we all have an Uncle Fluffy and a General of one kind or another within us. It also shows why we'll never get rid of them: There's no getting rid of our nervous system.

Walter Bradford Cannon is one of the most important names you've probably never heard. He was born in 1871 to a railroad worker and a high school teacher in Prairie du Chien, Wisconsin. After spending his youth obsessed with mammalian biology, he set out in 1892 for Harvard College with $182 in his pocket. Just six years later, as a Harvard Medical School student, he published his first study involving the use of X-ray technology to track the progress of a button through a dog's digestive system.

During that research, he noticed that when an animal in an experiment was frightened, the digestive muscle contractions in their stomach ceased. Curious, he observed a cascade of other physical changes coinciding with the digestive cessation. He writes, "These changes—the more rapid pulse, the deeper breathing, the increase of sugar in the blood, the secretion from the adrenal glands—were very diverse and seemed unrelated. Then, one wakeful night, after a considerable collection of these changes had been disclosed, the idea flashed through my mind that they could be nicely integrated if conceived as bodily preparations for supreme effort in flight or in fighting. Further investigation added to the collection and confirmed the general scheme suggested by the hunch."[4]

He published that "scheme" in his groundbreaking 1915 book, *Bodily Changes in Pain, Hunger, Fear and Rage*, and it is now commonly called the fight-or-flight response. It's the physiological reaction that happens when any animal feels threatened and the sympathetic branch of its autonomic nervous system kicks in, preparing it for a quick burst of reactivity. The adrenal glands release stress hormones, including adrenaline and cortisol. Consequently, blood vessels constrict in areas of the body tasked with nonessential activities—when your life is being threatened, your body deprioritizes digesting that burger from lunch. In contrast, blood vessels dilate in the muscles, preparing them for intense physical exertion. In the lungs, tiny air tubes called bronchioles also dilate to increase airflow. Pupils dilate to improve vision. The liver releases glucose into the bloodstream, creating a surplus of instant energy. Heart rate and blood pressure rapidly increase.

When your emotional heart is closing, your physical heart is entering fight-or-flight mode.

"So, what's wrong with that?" a client once asked me. "That's what we're supposed to do when we're threatened, right?"

"True. When threatened with mortal danger, your body is designed to fight or flee, but your wife was just wondering why you don't put down the toilet seat."

"Good point," he conceded. "But I didn't really fight or flee," he persisted. "I just made the case that nine times out of ten I do put it down, though she only notices the one time I don't."

"True again," I said. "That's because we human beings, with our fancy frontal lobes, have evolved a third way of responding to a threat. We try to manage it. Control it. Fix it. Solve it. Debate it. We try to neutralize it with our cognitive and verbal abilities. A better descriptor of the reaction for us sapiens would be the fight-flight-or-finagle response."

In other words, when you notice your heart is closing and you still struggle to slow down the closing, give yourself some grace—your nervous system is telling you that you're about to be annihilated, and it's gearing up to protect you. All mammals are wired to react immediately with one of two almost irresistible impulses: hide or fight. And we human beings have added a third: control. Thousands of years of evolution are working against you slowing down to contemplate how you want to respond.

No other creature on the planet pauses to ponder their panic.

You are entering deeply human territory here. You are trading out the impulsiveness that characterizes the rest of the animal kingdom for the awareness that distinguishes the human condition. You are transitioning from instantaneous action to intentional observation. You are watching your defenses instead of wielding them.

This is exceptionally difficult at first.

You'll see a defensive impulse rise up, you'll have second thoughts about acting on it, and then you might act on it anyway. At one level, this may feel like a failure. At another level, though, it's a powerful learning experience. The moment you thought, *I don't want to do that*, you located yourself outside the defensive urge, for perhaps the first time in your life. You untethered yourself from your protection, if just for a moment. That's a start.

Now, we want to expand that window in which you're able to watch it rather than wield it.

The Nine Most Common Closed-Hearted Defenses

Imagine it's Memorial Day in America.

You've gotten together with an old friend for a late-morning cup of coffee before the afternoon barbecues begin. You're not just old friends—you've been *best* friends. You grew up on the same block as kids, got into the same trouble, attended the same grade school, and double-dated together in high school. You see the world the same way and, even though it's been a minute since you've been together, you pick up right where you left off, as always.

Until their nonchalant comment about the holiday makes it clear they voted for the *other* presidential candidate last November.

When you were young that would have been no big deal, but it was a different America back then—one in which political rivals still worked together for the benefit of the country. The America you live in now has become deeply divided along party lines by social media algorithms that promote rage and hate and conflict. Almost everyone has taken a side, and you are shocked to discover your dear friend is sleeping with the enemy.

You are instantly triggered.

If Walter Bradford Cannon had his X-ray on you, he'd see the digestive contractions in your stomach come to a dead stop. You can feel a very unpleasant balloon expanding in the middle of your chest. Your heart is closing, and you will almost surely have a chance to watch one or more of the most common closed-hearted defenses arise within you. They fall into three categories, corresponding to the flight-fight-or-finagle response: hiding, fighting, and controlling (see fig. 2.1).

Hiding

Our hiding defenses develop earliest in life—typically between the ages of eight to twelve—so they tend to be simpler

Figure 2.1

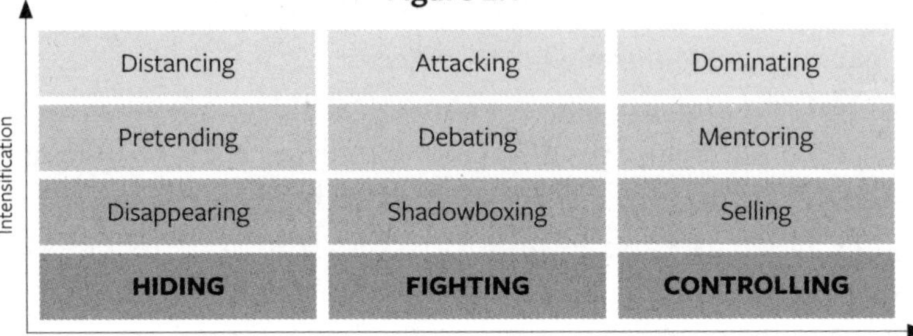

and less sophisticated than our other defenses. Hiding is about avoiding danger. Furthermore, while most animals wait until they're threatened to flee danger, human beings can anticipate a threat. We don't just flee from something that *is* happening, we hide from things that *may* happen. Here are three of the most common kinds of human hiding.

1. *Disappearing*. If your first reaction to your friend's comment is to gloss over it while suppressing your honest response, you're likely experiencing the disappearing defense. This is the grasshopper defense. At first, you just hold really still, hoping your natural coloring will help you blend into the background. Nothing to see here, move along! Or you might quickly hop to another subject to get away from this one. "I've always loved this holiday, especially getting together with my family for a barbecue. Did I mention my mom is pre-cancerous?"

Human beings camouflage themselves in countless ways: keeping the peace by keeping ourselves quiet, keeping our opinions to ourselves, keeping our feelings bottled up, and keeping our uniqueness under wraps, to name just a few. Disappearing is about avoiding attention because, theoretically, if someone doesn't see you, they aren't a threat to you. We neutralize the danger that comes with being different by disappearing altogether.

2. *Pretending*. Or perhaps your friend drops their political friendship bomb, and you reflexively say, "Oh my gosh, I know,

right?" The words are out of your mouth before you know it. They don't really mean anything substantive, but they leave a definite impression: You are in agreement. This is the chameleon defense. You anticipate a threat coming and momentarily change your colors to match the environment.

The key difference between disappearing and pretending is the shift from passively hiding who we are to actively pretending we're something we're not. Disappearing is peacemaking-lite, while pretending is the full peacemaking package. When we're in the pretending defense, we're giving more energy to crafting an acceptable persona than to cultivating genuine connection.

3. Distancing. Getting up from the table would feel more like confrontation than discontinuation, so you don't do that. Instead, you think to yourself, *Well, I guess this friendship is over. Decades right down the drain. What a shame*. You smile and go on with the conversation, but your heart has closed—it may look like you're still there, but really you're already gone.

Distancing most closely resembles the flight of other mammals, though we human beings have added many methods of distancing to our arsenal. Muting someone on social media. Removing yourself from a text thread. Leaving someone unread on Snapchat. I'll never forget the time I texted my wife and my text bubble had turned from blue to green. She'd blocked me. The distancing defense.

At its extreme, distancing leads to the death of relationships. To be clear, it's okay for relationships to end. Some endings are necessary, even inevitable. But it's always possible to end them by showing up authentically rather than disappearing defensively.

Fighting

By middle school, most young people are developing their more aggressive impulses—their fighting defenses. Fighting represents a shift from avoiding danger to becoming dangerous.

Of course, while we human beings still sometimes act upon our most aggressive animal impulses, our fighting defenses are usually crafted with civility in mind.

4. *Shadowboxing*. You let your friend's comment pass, but that night you find yourself lying in bed replaying the conversation in your mind, imagining what you could have said, brainstorming the perfect text to show them the error of their ways. The next morning, you actually write an email, but then you let it sit there in your drafts, gathering digital dust. This may look a little like hiding, but it's not. The energy of hiding is about moving away from the threat, whereas the energy of shadowboxing is about mentally moving toward the threat with your metaphorical gloves up.

Passive aggression is a form of shadowboxing that can happen even in the presence of the other. It's basically fighting with a dash of plausible deniability. We might sulk but say we're fine or be snide but insist we're being funny. Purposeful procrastination. Backhanded compliments. Subtly sabotaging cooperation. We might even forge alliances that work in our favor. Instead of sending the email, you text a third friend: "You're never going to guess what I found out yesterday!" If you think you aren't ever passive-aggressive, you may be the most skilled shadowboxer of all.

5. *Debating*. You step out of the shadows—perhaps not all the way, but a little—by offering a counterpoint to your friend's comment about the holiday. You're proud of how you do it too. You sound well-informed and well-reasoned. If you're not careful, you could start to sound a little defensive, but you'll be careful.

Of course, speaking up for yourself is a good thing, and it can be done with an open heart. However, debating is not authentic conversation—it's a rebuttal disguised as dialogue. Instead of learning how to be connected across the divide of differences, you're trying to coax the other person to your side of the divide.

Most of what looks like civil discourse on social media falls into this category of defense. At its best, it's closed-heartedness dressed up as open-mindedness. At its worst, it devolves into a relatively thin-skinned defense of one's own opinions, perspectives, or worldview. It toes the line of attacking the other person but never crosses it.

6. *Attacking*. "You've got to be kidding me!" you exclaim in response to your friend's disclosure of political affiliation. Of course, you know your friend isn't joking. In fact, they seem quite serious. That's what makes this so dumbfounding. You view that whole half of the country as rotten and corrupt, but your friend's presence in their camp throws a wrench in that judgment. Will you cast your friend as scum, as well, or will you open your heart to other possibilities? When the attacking defense is triggered, you'll cast your friend as scum and may even tell them so.

At this most visible end of the fighting spectrum, we start saying things we may regret once our heart is open again. We may even start *doing* things as the defense escalates into physical form. Will Smith's General, for instance, walked up onstage and physically attacked Chris Rock, slapping him across his face.

Controlling

Controlling is a step beyond avoiding danger or becoming dangerous: It's a more sophisticated way of trying to *manage* danger. This defense usually solidifies in our midtwenties, right around the time our brain finishes maturing. Most of us aren't control freaks, but many of us are control *sneaks*. In fact, we're so sneaky about it we're often not even aware of it ourselves.

7. *Selling*. Your friend voted for the other candidate. If not handled delicately, this could become a relationship-ending rift, and that would be tragic—you've been besties since way back when school field trips felt like an adventure and summer

vacations felt like forever. "So, what exactly do you love about them?" you ask. You sound like a used-car salesman asking, "So, what is your budget for a monthly payment?" It's the first step in a line of Socratic questioning you hope will end with genuine connection on your terms. It won't work, though, for a very specific reason.

You can either have an agenda or you can connect, but you can't do both.

Oftentimes, we come to a conversation with something we want to get *from* it, rather than simply showing up *to* it. We want approval, an apology, help, or the dishwasher loaded correctly. We want to be prioritized. We want to have fun. We want our employees to produce more. We want a lot of things, and most of them are totally okay to want, as long as we simply say them instead of subtly selling them.

8. Mentoring. "Where have you been getting your news?" Theoretically, this could be a genuine, openhearted question in response to your friend's proclamation of political alliance. When you're in mentoring mode, however, it's the first closed-hearted question in a diagnostic interview. Something is clearly wrong with them. You're going to identify it for them and help them fix it. You will mentor them back to the correct path, which just so happens to coincide with your worldview.

If you feel you must fix someone before you can be with them, you're probably in the mentoring defense.

"Cure without care," writes Catholic author Henri J. M. Nouwen, "makes us into rulers, controllers, manipulators, and prevents a real community from taking shape. Cure without care makes us preoccupied with quick changes, impatient and unwilling to share each other's burden. And so cure can often become offending instead of liberating."[5]

Cure is mentorship, while care is membership.

9. Dominating. "You have to promise me you will never do that again," you say emphatically to your friend, stabbing your finger at them. When we cross the line from trying to influence our people to actually dictating what they are allowed to do and say, we've crossed the line into the most intense category of controlling defense. Most of us can't identify with being a dictator, but most of us can be dictatorial from time to time. If you start to rely on dominating as a defense, you'll start to monitor your people's movements, restrict their behavior, and punish them for operating outside of spoken or unspoken guidelines set up by you.

Will Smith shouted at Chris Rock to keep Jada's name out of his mouth before walking up on stage and slapping him. It was Will's attempt to dominate Rock by telling him what he could and could not say. Rock smiled back. Will's dominating defense didn't work, so he shifted to attacking. This is actually quite common: Closed-heartedness often devolves into less sophisticated forms as it persists—dominating often devolves into attacking, which often devolves into distancing.

Confessing Instead of Conquering

Now imagine it's the evening of March 27, 2022. At the Dolby Theater in Hollywood, the 94th Academy Awards are well underway. Chris Rock makes a hurtful joke about Jada's alopecia, a chronic condition resulting in hair loss and baldness. Will is prepared for this moment, though. All of his personal work has paid off. He's learned to love not just his inner beauty but all the defenses he's devised to protect it. So, he's been aware of both his opening and his closing all night long. For example, he's been noticing his mentoring defense in all its glory—the part of him that feels on top of the world and wants to bestow his wisdom on everyone below him.

Chris Rock's joke hits home. Will's cortisol spikes. Walter Bradford Cannon's fight-or-flight response kicks in. Will's appetite disappears instantaneously. His muscles are flooded with oxygenated blood. His vision crystallizes to 30/20. Every fiber of his being is fueled by a wave of sugar pushed into the bloodstream by his liver. He's ready to act. *More* than ready.

Instead, he watches it from the seat of his awareness.

He notices his mentoring defense give way to Uncle Fluffy, his first form of hiding from the violence in his parents' marriage. He laughs at the joke along with everyone else—the good-natured little boy keeping the peace by staying playful. His heart hammers in his chest. He looks to his left, where Jada is *not* smiling. He sees that pretending wasn't enough to keep this train on the tracks tonight. He watches as his dominating defense takes over. The General wants to scream at Chris Rock. Will's temples pulse. He wants to get out of his chair and do something about it. His attacking defense.

Instead—rooted in a sense that he is not his most powerful protective impulses but rather the part of him *observing* those impulses—he remains aware of his defenses instead of acting defensive. Knowing he can't open up by *conquering* his closed heart but by *confessing* his closed heart, he leans over to Jada and whispers in her ear, "The General wants to go up there and slap that fool."

Jada smiles a small smile and pecks him on the cheek. "Tell the General thanks but let him know this night is about you and your award, not his beef with that stooge."

And the night moves on, ending in a very different acceptance speech from the Academy Award Winner for Best Actor, Will Smith.

Perhaps I'm just fantasizing about a parallel universe in which my childhood hero doesn't fall so hard from the pedestal we all put him on. Perhaps this is just the perfectionism of my own mentoring defense sneaking onto the page. There's probably a little truth in that. But there's a bigger truth too. I've been watching myself for years now, and I've been watching my clients watch themselves for years too. And this is what

I've seen: There's no such thing as a perfect world, but a more peaceful world is well within our watchful reach.

Exercise: Categorize Your Closing

After a handful of appointments, Henry and Sarah are catching their hearts closing earlier and earlier. Henry is noticing his heart twinge closed every time Sarah makes a less than positive comment. Sarah says her heart subtly shuts every time Henry glosses over something "real." They haven't had a big fight in weeks.

During our next appointment, I present them with the Disrupt Your Defensiveness Grid and ask them to become black boxes once again, recording a new piece of data: which defenses show up around the moment of their closing. Finally, I ask them to email me before our next appointment with their observations so we can use the time to complete an exercise together.

Henry emails me first:

> Hey Doc,
>
> I would have told you I'm more of a fighter, but I've been watching myself hide a lot when my heart closes. I almost tell Sarah about my work stress, but I don't do it. I just tell her everything was great. Pretending. Anxiety in my chest when that happens. Not sure why. I've got a thing for luxury watches and I don't tell her I bought one. I just wear it, and when she finally notices it, I tell her I've had it for a while. More pretending. Not sure why I do that either.
>
> Mostly, though, I do the distancing thing you talked about. I just shut down when she starts to go dark. I nod along for a while and then find some excuse to get out of the conversation. She's got a lot of issues from her childhood, and it's her job to deal with those. She needs to learn how to love herself so she can be happy. But she doesn't want my help with that. Believe me, I've tried. So it just makes sense for me to stay in my own lane and let her stay in hers.

Probably not what you wanted to hear, but it's what I recorded, so there you go. See you soon.

Sarah emails me the morning of our next appointment:

Dear Dr. Kelly,

I told you I'd see a lot of hiding, but I actually do a lot of shadowboxing too. On Saturday we had an end of the school year block party, and Henry wanted to go mountain biking with some neighbors in the morning. I knew I'd get no help with the kids while I was trying to prepare for the party. I just kept thinking, "He's a selfish jerk," over and over again.

I realized I was doing it though, so I laid out the schedule for him and gave him a chance to change his own mind about the bike ride, but he was totally oblivious. So, guess what? I called him a selfish jerk! It wasn't until my attacking defense showed up that I realized I'd been shadowboxing all morning.

I make a note that neither of them identified their controlling defenses, though both emails revealed some significant controlling impulses. Henry, for instance, shows a mentoring mentality toward Sarah. He sees her as having problems she needs to fix and admits to trying to persuade her to fix them. In fact, with a single email, Henry has articulated his entire closed-hearted arc: Try to change her first (mentoring), fight about it when she refuses (attacking), and then give up on connection when that goes nowhere (distancing).

Sarah, on the other hand, is even sneakier about her attempt to control Henry. She approached the conversation about the morning bike ride with an agenda: selling him on helping her prep for the block party. He either didn't know he was being sold to, or he refused to buy. For Sarah, too, when her attempt to subtly control the situation wasn't successful, she resorted to fighting.

They're ready for the Closed-Hearted Conflict Cycle template.

It's a single-page PDF that depicts a cyclone. At the center of the cyclone is space to write an event that triggered a conflict cycle. Then the cycle spirals outward from there in a sequence of steps, each consisting of a person's name, their behavior, their level of closed-heartedness from one to ten, and the type of defense that was implemented at that step, if applicable. It can be used to map out the progression of your closed-hearted defenses in any interaction.

I begin the next appointment with Henry and Sarah by reviewing their emails and bringing awareness to the controlling defenses in their blind spots.

"Yeah," Henry admits as openheartedly as I've ever seen him, "I suppose it wouldn't feel great to have someone trying to fix you all the time."

Sarah, too, is openhearted. "I get it. If I want something, I need to set him up for success by being direct."

Next, I introduce the conflict cycle template and ask if they've had any recent conflicts we could map out. Henry smirks. Sarah nods and says, "Dinner last night. Owen spilled his milk and it went south pretty fast."

"How so?" I ask.

"All I did was sigh," she explains. "I wasn't even upset or closed-hearted or anything. I was probably at an eight. I was just tired. And Henry started lecturing me before I could even get to the paper towels."

"Perfect. Let's start with that." I share my tablet to the Zoom screen and at the center of the cyclone write, *Sarah sighs over spilled milk.*

"How did Henry react?" I ask her.

"He said, and I quote, 'It's not that big of a deal—no need to cry over spilled milk.'"

"I was just being positive," Henry protests. "I even said it nicely!"

I redirect him. "Henry, if you'd tuned in to your heart in that moment, is it possible it was already closing?"

There's a pregnant pause. Henry's brow furrows the way it does.

"Dang, Doc," he says eventually. "Yeah. I went from a ten to a six just like that. I could tell she was going to go dark and I wanted to keep things light."

"Which defense kicked in at that moment?" I ask.

"Mentoring," he admits, grimacing.

In the next step of the cyclone, I write, *Henry, Says it's not a big deal, 6, Mentoring.*

It doesn't take long to fill in the rest of the cyclone.

Sarah, Refuses to wipe up the milk, 5, Distancing.

Henry, Cracks a joke about having to do Sarah's domestic duties for her, 5, Passive-aggressive shadowboxing.

Sarah, Imagines her various retorts while staying quiet, 3, Shadowboxing.

Henry, Cleans up the mess while saying Sarah needs to grow up, 3, Attacking.

Sarah, Tells him to apologize or he's sleeping on the couch, 2, Dominating.

Henry, Disposes of the wet paper towels and leaves the house, 1, Distancing.

"Your job next time," I say, "will be to fill in the cyclone before it happens. You both know the script all too well by now. So, when you first feel your heart start to close, fill in what's coming next. Do it together if you're able to stay open enough, and if you can't stay open enough, we'll talk about what comes next."

What comes next is calming themselves before connecting themselves.

3

Cultivate Calmness Before Connectedness

When we are unable to find tranquility within ourselves, it is useless to seek it elsewhere.

François de La Rochefoucauld

"Dad, I'm standing outside in the rain. Where are you?"

It's the kind of December night that feels lost somewhere between autumn and winter, with raindrops so cold you wish they were snow. Daylight saving time ended a few weeks ago, so at five o'clock it's already dark. The headlights passing me are just bleary orbs in the downpour.

I'm picking up my son Quinn from basketball practice, and I'm a couple minutes late. Nevertheless, I figure he's playfully pranking me from the dry confines of the school—why would he be standing outside in this weather? I prepare my own witty reply, but it goes to waste because, when I pull up to the school, he is actually standing in the rain, drenched.

Something is very off here.

Quinn gets in the car. He's generally a happy kid. It's been years since I've seen him overcome by something other than smiles. Now, distress is wafting off him in waves. My whole being clenches. The pilot light in my nervous system ignites.

"What's up, bud?" I ask, doing my best impersonation of a calm father.

He tries to speak while choking down emotion, and they cancel each other out. I'm forced to wait in impotent silence. I admonish myself to relax. After all, I don't really know anything yet, so why get so bent out of shape? Nevertheless, my nervous system rumbles like a furnace before it kicks on, and I want to shake him until some explanation comes tumbling out. Instead, I wait, my knuckles white on the wheel.

Finally, he's ready to speak.

"Before practice I told Coach I'd have to miss this Friday's game so I can play in the band concert, and Coach asked if I like band more than basketball." He takes a deep breath. "I told him it wasn't my decision, that you and Mom are making me go to band because it's for a grade. Then," he says, the briefest of smiles back in his voice, "I went out and had the best practice of my life. I was so proud of myself, Dad. But . . ."

He trails off, emotion once again winning the war over words. My nervous system redlines, the furnace now running full blast. I can barely stand to stay in my own skin. He gathers himself to finish the story.

"Then Coach brought us into a circle at the end of practice, and he said anyone who skips a game can expect to lose their spot in the rotation, and some of us clearly care about the team and some of us don't, and everybody will know who is who."

Reliving it is too much for Quinn's natural joy to withstand. He grows quiet as his emotions have the final say in the conversation.

I guess he's got to skip the concert and go to the game, I think. I'm willing to do anything to prevent his shunning. Then, *Wait a second! We're not going to reinforce these tactics.* I try to keep the trembling anger out of my voice when I speak next. I fail. My words warble.

"This is what happened, bud. Before practice, your coach wanted you at the game, but after he saw how well you played during practice, he *really* wanted you at the game. So he's trying to shame you into changing your mind, and we're not going to play along with that."

"Well, what are we going to do? My teammates are going to hate me!"

I know exactly what I *want* to do. I want to turn the car around, find his coach, and punch him in the nose. I don't, though. Not because I'm some paragon of virtue. His coach is twice my size and half my age, and I'd get my butt kicked.

We pull into the driveway, and Quinn makes a beeline for his bedroom, bypassing his mom. She asks for an explanation, and I give it to her. She's the best kind of mother bear, and her roar mingles with mine. I decide I'm going to have the coach's career on a platter. I whip out my laptop and open an email to the administration.

"Where do I start?" I ask her.

"By regulating yourself," she says. "Then, when you're calm, write what's on your heart." She's right.

A reaction is a failure of self-regulation, while a response is the fruit of self-regulation.

Looking for Regulation in All the Wrong Places

It's tempting to portray my dysregulated reaction to Quinn's predicament as the understandable urges of a caring father. There's plenty of truth to it: I love Quinn fiercely, and I want to protect him from harm.

The rest of the truth is a little harder to face: Much of what we call love is really just an attempt to feel calm inside.

That may sound selfish at first, but it's not, really. It's a natural instinct built into our biology over time. The human organism is the pinnacle of a self-regulating system designed to maintain an internal state of safety and satisfaction. Any disruption to this homeostasis is immediately noted and automatically addressed. For our nervous system, it's not a question of selfishness, it's a matter of survival.

Without our "selfishness," we're not here.

When Quinn got in the car and it became clear something was wrong, my nervous system's fight-flight-or-finagle response was triggered, and everything that followed was an attempt to calm it down. For example, my first impulse was controlling. I wanted to regulate my nervous system by forcing information from him. The dominating defense. My second impulse was to hide—I considered regulating my nervous system by sending Quinn to the basketball game instead of the band concert. The pretending defense. My third impulse was to fight, first with fists and then with words. The attacking defense.

The biggest problem with these self-regulating reactions isn't that they're selfish. It's that they're exceptionally inefficient.

Imagine the interior walls of your home are painted a shade of green that reminds you of sewage and makes you nauseous every time you set foot inside the house. The home has endured a lot of wear and tear, so the walls are badly scratched and scuffed. It's just not very relaxing to be in your home. So, you buy all the necessary supplies to repaint the interior, and you make your preparations: taping the trim, covering the floors and furniture, and stirring the new paint. It's a pastel yellow hue that feels like springtime turning into summertime and reminds you of the curtains that rustled in the breeze at your grandmother's country house when you were young. Finally, you're ready to repaint your home in a calming color.

Then, you walk out of the house, track down everyone who's ever been in the house, and tell them what they need to do in order for you to repaint your walls.

You start with your wife, who's out in the garden. You reiterate that if she could just appreciate everything you contribute to the family and quit nagging you for more, the walls will repaint themselves. Or perhaps you find your husband in the garage, tinkering as always with one senseless project or another, and tell him again that if he could just slow down and give you an ounce of quality time, the walls will repaint themselves. Then you get in the car and track down your teenager at her high school and explain that if she could just avoid bad friends, a drinking problem, and premarital pregnancy, the walls will repaint themselves. At your parents' house, you suggest to them—okay, a touch passive-aggressively—that if they'd apologize for being so distracted or fragile or authoritarian or downright traumatizing during your childhood, then your walls will repaint themselves. Finally, you spend the rest of the afternoon working through your list of exes, friends past and present, work colleagues, bosses, and that humiliating gym teacher from the seventh grade, telling each of them what you need to hear for your walls to be repainted in a calming color.

Exhausted from your busy day, you pull into the driveway, walk into your home, and flip on the lights. To your dismay, the walls are still painted the same nauseating green. Not to mention, you've now got a splitting headache after listening to everyone defend themselves all day. You kick off your shoes in frustration. One of them hits the wall, adding a new scuff to the existing constellation there. It's so defeating. How in the world are you ever going to get these walls repainted when no one will cooperate with your project?

You'll try to get a good night's sleep and start again tomorrow.

As a metaphor, this is absurd, of course. If we wanted the walls of our house repainted in a more calming color, we wouldn't leave the house and try to change other people or the past or situations that are totally out of our control. We'd just start painting. Yet, this is essentially what we do all the time in our attempts to regulate our nervous system and calm our interior world. We take an unnecessary and unproductive detour through other people on the journey of emotional regulation, and then we call our travels "love."

Love isn't connecting with others to calm ourselves, it's calming ourselves to connect with others.

A Revolution in Calming

When I arrived at Penn State University in the fall of 1999 to begin my doctoral training, the field of psychology was in the midst of a scientific revolution.

The previous thirty years of psychological treatment had been dominated by cognitive behavioral therapy (CBT). In contrast to its predecessor—behaviorism, which was only interested in exterior actions—CBT argued that the interior life is an important dimension of human functioning. It's a concept we now take for granted as much as we do seat belts and bottled water and *Saturday Night Live*. Specifically, CBT posited that dysfunctional behaviors stem from incorrect thinking. For instance, if you could "restructure" your incorrect thoughts about danger, then you could eliminate your anxiety and therefore more easily change your behaviors.

Research proved that CBT was helpful, but just a little.

Then, around the time I got to graduate school, a new wave of thinking swept through the field of psychology. It drew upon concepts like mindfulness and acceptance. A quarter century later, it's now referred to broadly as mindfulness-based cognitive therapy (MBCT), and it focuses less on the content of our thoughts and more on our relationship to them. Essentially, it posits that our suffering does not stem from the nature of our thinking but from our resistance to it. Instead of wasting our time trying to eliminate or change the thoughts and sensations of our inner life, we can learn to live peacefully with them.

Well ahead of his time, President Abraham Lincoln exemplified this philosophy when he said, "Do I not destroy my enemies when I make them my friends?"[1] The new psychological paradigm drew upon the same wisdom—it was not about correcting our thoughts and feelings but about befriending them. This, it turns out, helps a lot.

An old Eastern parable illustrates why.

- - -

A spiritual teacher is confronted one morning in his meditation hut by one of his students. "Teacher," he says, "you have been training me for a year, and yet I still have all the same terrible thoughts and still feel all the same terrible feelings. When will I be free of this? When will I finally have peace?"

The teacher is unsurprised. Many years ago, he asked these questions of his own teacher.

"Get a handful of salt and a cup of water and return to me," he instructs the student.

The student returns holding a palmful of salt in one hand and a cup in the other. "Now, pour the salt into the water." The student does so.

"Now, drink the water."

The student once again follows the teacher's instructions, pausing halfway through with a grimace on his face before finishing the rest.

"What was it like to drink the water?" the teacher asks.

"It was terrible," the student says. "It was almost impossible to drink."

The teacher nods. "Now, go get another handful of salt." The student returns, palm up, holding the salt.

"Follow me," says the teacher, rising slowly, grabbing his cane, and exiting the hut. He picks his way slowly down a path that ends at an expansive, crystal clear lake. He points at the lake. "Now, pour the salt in the lake." The student does so.

"Now cup your hands and drink from the lake."

The student bends down, ladles some water with his hands, and drinks it down.

"What was it like to drink the water?" he asks a second time.

"It was quite refreshing," the student says cautiously.

The teacher nods. "Quit trying to rid yourself of the salt in you. Instead, become the lake."

In this story, the salt represents our inner turmoil. Our anxiety. Our anger. Our agitation. Our stress. Our dysregulated nervous system in its many forms. The water represents our consciousness, our awareness, our capacity to coexist with these inner experiences. To welcome them. To soften toward them. Like Lincoln said, to befriend them. Most of us are like that student, though: We spend a lot of time trying to diminish the salt and almost no time diluting it.

Here are a few of the ways we get caught up in the old paradigm of salt removal:

First, like the house painter above, we blame other people for our saltiness and demand they do something to dispel it. This is the reaction my wife was encouraging me to restrain as I blamed Quinn's coach for my saltiness and almost demanded that the school board remove the salt from me by removing the coach from his position. Trying to force other people to remove the salt from our glass is a delusional way to deal with our saltiness, and usually adds more salt than it removes.

Second, CBT prevailed for several decades because it does put the salt in a better perspective. If your nervous system is acting like you're about to be eaten by a lion on the Serengeti, it helps to remind yourself that you're actually in your bedroom in rural Illinois and are just a little worked up about your son being treated unfairly. The limitations of this technique are palpable, though—sure, this situation isn't as salty as some other situations, but you still don't want to drink *this* one down.

Third, there is a range of relaxation practices at our disposal; breathing exercises in particular are a popular method for making it less salty inside. Deep breathing. Box breathing. Wim Hoff breathing. When done correctly, these exercises can activate the parasympathetic nervous system, which helps to neutralize the fight-or-flight arousal of the sympathetic nervous system.

In my reading chair, I open an app on my phone and pick a popular breathing exercise. It starts to help.

Until it doesn't.

When you engage in any relaxation practice with the intention of removing your salt altogether, as soon as the so-called solution begins to feel like it's not "working," your water gets even saltier. There's a reason for that. When you fight your salt, you aren't terminating the fight-or-flight reaction, you're simply turning it inward against your own thoughts and feelings. It's like trying to remove the salt you just added to the glass of water by throwing more salt into the glass. This is the limitation of any intervention that pretends it can remove the salt altogether and forever.

What we need is not a better method but a better intention.

Become a Larger Lake

Mindfulness-based approaches set a better intention. They don't seek to eliminate the salt, they seek to make you a bigger container for the salt. As mindfulness guru Jon Kabat-Zinn says, "You can't stop the waves, but you can learn to surf."[2]

As the relaxation exercise fails to calm me down, I'm reminded of a morning several years earlier when I was sitting in the very same chair. It had become clear my collarbone wasn't healing properly, so my doctor prescribed daily ultrasound bone stimulation at home. I'd sit in the chair with the medical device attached to my shoulder, not knowing if it was working at all. During that time, I explored different meditations in the hopes of dispelling my distress about the unhealed injury.

One morning, I came across a meditation that startled me.

First, the guide instructed us to locate the greatest discomfort in our body. I focused on my shoulder, having done enough meditations to know what was coming next: He'd tell us to breathe into the discomfort, release it, and relax it instead. I knew it wouldn't work—my shoulder was going to throb no matter how much I breathed "into" it. However, the guide didn't suggest getting rid of the salt.

"And if you notice any areas of tension," he said, "just [allow] them to be here. So often we want to change what we find."[3]

Instantly, I was no longer in a losing battle to let go of my pain, and that felt freeing. Instead, I was able to approach it. To be with it. To bear witness to it. To live like a larger lake, if you will, holding it in awareness, simply letting it be the salt that it was. The pain was still there, but like salt in a lake, it was diluted now. The moment was more drinkable. During that ultrasound session, I went on to develop my own self-regulation exercise, which combines the most effective elements of traditional breathing methods with the more helpful intentions of mindfulness approaches.

I call it the Margin for Terror visualization, which I will explain in more detail at the end of this chapter.

At the beginning of my openhearted journey, it took me days of practicing the visualization to become a bigger container for my broken shoulder. By the day of Quinn's basketball practice, though, I've been practicing it regularly for two years, and I'm able to become a larger lake relatively quickly. Within just a few minutes, I'm peacefully coexisting with the whole range of reactions to his coach. And once my nervous system is regulated, I'm flexible and free to see options beyond hiding, attacking, or controlling. Now that I'm calm, I simply want to speak up on behalf of who Quinn is. So, this is what I write:

> Dear Coach,
>
> Quinn would prefer that I not be sending this to you, but as his father I feel compelled to support him.
>
> Quinn is fully committed to basketball, and he has a track record of being fiercely loyal to his coaches and his teammates. He's the kind of player that will die for you.
>
> As his parent, I have the difficult task of supporting both his passions and his commitments, and while he is most passionate about basketball, he did commit to the band for one year. This Friday night is one of only two band performances this semester, and it factors into his semester grade, which will have a lasting impact on his academic future. Therefore, I made the decision to require his attendance at the band concert. I was proud of the maturity he showed in both accepting this decision from his authority figures and taking responsibility for it by communicating it to you directly.
>
> He came out of practice tonight devastated that your belief in him may have been damaged by our decision. I hope your view of him will not be diminished by it. Thanks for hearing me out, and I'd be happy to talk more about it.

I show the email to Quinn, telling him he can veto it, and because I don't need anything more to feel calm, I'm totally okay if he does. At first, he says no, but by the time dinner rolls around, he's changed his mind and gives it the green light. I send the email, and we eat. Then, after dinner, while doing dishes, another idea emerges from my open heart. Quinn is still sitting at the table, tapping out something on his phone.

"Hey, bud," I say, "you could message your teammates and explain the situation to them. You know, remind them of who you are, like we did with your coach."

Without looking up, Quinn replies, "That's what I'm doing right now."

His teammates immediately reply with their vote of confidence in him, and, twelve hours later, his coach replies to my email with a level of ownership that brings tears to my wife's eyes. In the years that follow, he'll become one of Quinn's favorite coaches of all time.

"Regulation is the key to creating a safe connection," writes world-renowned psychiatrist and childhood trauma expert Bruce Perry. "Without some degree of regulation, it is difficult to connect with another person, and without connection, there is minimal reasoning. Regulate, relate, then reason."[4]

In other words, calm yourself to connect yourself. Not the other way around.

Exercise: Margin for Terror Visualization

It's been several weeks since our last call and, when Henry and Sarah appear on my screen, it's not in two windows but one. Their smiles and easy energy suggest the conversation I'm interrupting is a pleasant one.

"Well, this is a first," I say. "You're in the same room for our call today."

"It's important to Sarah that I prioritize these calls," says Henry, "so I blocked an hour on my calendar before and after these meetings. We're getting lunch afterward." Sarah leans into him, their shoulders touching.

"Any plans for the weekend?" I ask.

When it comes to the triggering of our nervous systems, there are land mines everywhere, even in innocent questions about your weekend.

"Yep," says Sarah. "I've been wanting to go hiking as a family at this one state park, and something always gets in the way. Last time it rained cats and dogs. But this Sunday the forecast is perfect, and our calendar is clear, so we're packing a picnic and spending the day there." As she speaks, the smile slides right off Henry's face. Sarah hasn't noticed yet.

"Henry," I say, "it looks like you might have something to add?"

She leans away, turns toward him, and when she sees the look on his face, her smile evaporates too. "What is it?" she demands, her face flushing with adrenaline.

His jaw does that clamping thing before he opens his mouth to speak. "I moved my flight up from Monday to Sunday morning. The guy I'm meeting with asked me to play a round of golf with his business partner on Sunday afternoon before we meet on Monday. He said it'll basically guarantee the deal. Our calendar was clear, so I booked it. We're going to have to do the hike another time."

Sarah opens her mouth to speak. Closes it. Opens it again. Closes it again. She crosses her arms across her chest as she turns back to the screen. "Fine," she says. "I'll go with the kids on my own and take lots of pictures and send them to you while you're on your stupid golf course and you'll see how much you're missing and how much we don't need you." She scoffs at herself. "I suppose I'm attacking, but I don't care."

"Sounds like it," I confirm. "Any other defensive urges showing up?"

"Oh yeah," she says without hesitation. "I definitely want to mentor right now. I want to tell him he's got serious issues and I want to list them all out and tell him what he needs to do to fix them and make sure he knows that if he doesn't, he's going to regret the life he's chosen to live."

It's a new benchmark for the angriest I've ever seen her. Henry's jaw is still clamped, but his face has become expressionless, and he's reclined as far as the chair will go.

"And Henry," I ask, "how about you?"

"I want to reschedule my flight to this afternoon instead of Sunday morning." Cold as ice.

"So, distancing?" I confirm. He nods reluctantly.

"Good," I say. "You're both doing a great job seeing the way your heart is closing." At that, Sarah's frustration turns toward me.

"This is where we get stuck. Ninety percent of the time it's good between us now, but this 10 percent completely cancels out the 90 percent. I *want* to open back up, but I can't imagine doing it."

I nod. "That's because your nervous system will always win. While it's acting like you're in danger, it will be impossible to open back up. So, we have to start by regulating it. I'd be happy to guide you through an exercise that might help. Sarah, would you be willing to go first?"

"Sure," she says, sounding exactly as enthused as I'd expect her to be. "But I don't think I can do it with him here."

That makes sense. It can be difficult to convince your nervous system it's not under threat in the presence of the thing it feels most threatened by at the moment, whether it's your spouse or your kid or a customer service representative insisting there is absolutely nothing they can do to serve you.

"Henry, what do you say? Would you be willing to let Sarah have the rest of the hour?"

Henry is more than willing to bow out and return to his office, leaving Sarah alone on my screen.

"Go ahead and close your eyes," I say. She does. "Now, locate the place in your body where you feel your closed heart the most right now." Pause. "Do you have it?" She nods. "Where is it?"

"In my chest," she says.

"Where in your chest?" I ask. "Can you put your hand directly over it?" She places her hand slightly left of center on her chest.

"Good. Now I'm going to ask you to describe that feeling to me in visual terms. Imagine I gave you a set of crayons and asked you to draw it on a piece of paper. What would it look like?"

This comes easier to some clients than others, but this mother of two young children has no trouble with it.

"It's a big ball of jagged black squiggles," she says emphatically.

"Good. Are there any other colors in it?

"It has sort of a red glow throughout but especially around the edges."

"Is it small or big inside of you?"

"It's small. But it's heavy."

"Is it static or does it move?" I ask. "Does it swirl or pulse, for instance?"

"It moves constantly and chaotically, like ants on an anthill."

"Is it hot or cold?"

She pauses for a while before answering. "It looks hot, but actually it's cold. Really cold. Like outer space."

"Okay, good. Now I want you to press your hand firmly down on that area in your chest. Come as close to that feeling in there as you can." Her arm shifts as she does so.

"Now, while keeping that in your mind's eye, I want you to notice that you're also breathing. Be mindful of the natural inflow and outflow of your breath. Don't do anything to it. Just notice it."

I pause, giving her some time to come to mindfulness in this way. She sinks a little deeper into her chair, her musculature already noticeably relaxing.

"Now, on your next in-breath, I want you to visualize the air entering into the space around your black squiggles, expanding that space like a lung so that you can see a wide margin between that feeling and everything else in there. Then release the air and let the margin disappear. Go ahead and do that now." She breathes long and slow. "Can you see it happening?" She nods.

"Continue breathing and visualizing like that for about a minute. The goal here is not to breathe into the feeling and relax it but to breathe around the feeling and let it be what it is." A minute passes.

"Now, on each out-breath, I want you to picture yourself leaving just a little more air around that feeling. Just the slimmest of margins. Just a bit of space around it that grows ever so slightly more spacious with each inhale and exhale." Another minute passes.

"Okay, now keep breathing until you feel peaceful enough to consider opening your heart again. This doesn't mean you have to—it just means you feel like you have a choice again. And it doesn't mean the black squiggles are gone. It means you know you are safe even though they are there. You can coexist with them. You can be connected in the midst of them, not in conflict because of them. When you feel you've gotten there, go ahead and open your eyes."

She breathes for several more minutes before slowly opening her eyes. She removes her hand from her chest and uses the back of it to wipe her eyes.

"What are you feeling?" I ask.

"All the red went out of the squiggles," she says quietly. "Now they're just black. I just feel . . . sad."

I don't know it at the time, but it's the last I'll see of Sarah for several months.

PART II

GET FREE

> Your vision will become clear only when you can look into your own heart. . . . Who looks outside dreams; who looks inside awakes.
>
> Carl Jung

4

Simplify the Solution

Yesterday I was clever, so I wanted to change the world.
Today I am wise, so I am changing myself.

Rumi

There's an old parable about someone rowing a boat across a lake in fog so thick they can barely see the bow of the boat. The fog muffles the morning sounds, and all is still. They're at peace. Suddenly, they're jarred by the bumping of their boat into another rowboat, and their equanimity is instantly erased.

"Why don't you watch where you're going?" they holler at the person in the other boat.

At just that moment, a breeze blows and the fog dissipates so they can see the other boat. They open their mouth to ask the accusatory question again, but the words get lost somewhere before their lips. The other boat is empty.

When our hearts close, we believe we're closing them to the person in the other boat, but what if we're not? What if we're closing our heart to the bumping of the boats? What if we're not closing to a *who*, but we're closing to a *what*? What if we're not actually in conflict with the person in front of us but with the experience that's been triggered inside of us?

The third-century Desert Fathers—the earliest Christian monastics—discovered this for themselves. They retreated from civilization to live in isolation in the Scetes desert of ancient Egypt. As another parable goes, a Desert Father would leave behind all the people who seemed to be triggering his unholy anger. Then, a couple days into his life of solitude, he'd stub his toe on a rock in the cave he was calling home and would discover with dismay that his anger had followed him to the desert.

We think we're reacting to people, but really we're reacting to pain.

Nobody Grants Pardons Right Before Lunch

A forgotten veggie burger can ruin a reunion.

It's the Fourth of July, and our home is teeming with family in town for the holiday. My wife has been running the grill, its aromas mingling with the sound of chattering people around the house, "God Bless the U.S.A." on the portable speaker, and firecrackers in the distance. Finally, she announces that the food is ready, and I direct everybody toward the kitchen island, which is barely visible beneath platters of meat, corn on the cob, watermelon, potato salad, coleslaw, and so on. Everyone loads a plate and finds a place around the house to eat. Finally, it's my turn to dish up.

I approach the tray of meat, where most of the hamburgers and bratwursts and chicken breasts have already been chosen. That's okay. I haven't eaten meat in twenty years. I'm looking for the perfect puck-shape of a plant-based patty. I scan the tray. Everything left has the uneven silhouette of hand-shaped beef. My heart sinks and my stomach growls.

"Uh-oh," I say to my wife. "Someone took the veggie burger."

A look passes over her face—some mixture of surprise, anguish, and . . . preparation. "No," she says slowly, "I forgot to make you one."

I'll be told later that none of our extended family noticed this interaction. However, for my three kids, it was like a needle had scratched across the record of our night. They stood still and watched me, soda cans paused halfway to their mouths, statuesque. They have ample experience with how badly this moment can break, like the Father's Day when my wife got me the wrong bagel from my favorite deli. I loved the deli's plain bagel with chocolate chip cream cheese. She got me a chocolate chip bagel with plain cream cheese, which I was not interested in at all.

I handled the minor mix-up . . . poorly.

I'm oblivious to their bated breath, however, as I stare down at my patty-less plate. Walter Bradford Cannon's fight-or-flight response is kicking into full gear. My heart thumps in my chest. Blood pulses in my ears. I consider a passive-aggressive reaction: histrionically slapping a double helping of potato salad onto the empty half of my plate in a great show of gastric martyrdom. Then, more aggressive impulses present themselves. I want to attack my wife's shortcomings. She's thoughtless and careless. Ungrateful and unkind. Delinquent in her duties.

It's absurd, I know.

On this night, she has single-handedly—and with true gladness of heart—made everyone feel at home. Not to mention, she's done it mostly for *my* extended family, who she treats like her own. She's remembered a million details and overlooked only one. At first glance, the math of my madness just doesn't add up. However, if there's one thing you learn as a psychologist, it's this: Everyone makes sense once you have all the data.

During my predoctoral internship at a veterans' hospital outside of Chicago, I was assigned a client with paranoid schizophrenia. She had a number of delusions, but one was particularly disruptive. She believed car headlights at night were lasers that would burn holes in her back if she didn't avoid them, so she couldn't leave the house after dark. Nothing could convince her otherwise.

For months, our sessions were standoffs—her not trusting me and me struggling to get through to her with the truth. Eventually, at a supervisor's suggestion, I quit trying to tug her into my reality and chose to join hers. I asked her what the headlights reminded her of. In a startling moment of transparency, she told me when she was a kid, her mother would get drunk at night, start smoking, and put the cigarettes out on her back. She lifted the back of her shirt and showed me constellations of scars. They might as well have been laser burns from headlights.

If you look closely enough, there's a rational reason for every irrational reaction.

Usually, though, we struggle to recognize the real reason for our reactions because we look for our explanations around us rather than within us. If you're a schizophrenic young woman afraid of the dark, you look around, see headlights, and blame them for your fear. Or, if you're that young woman's therapist a quarter century later, you feel your heart closing to a forgotten veggie burger, look around, see your wife, and blame her for the closing.

If you don't know *what* you're reacting to, you'll blame *who* you're reacting to.

This feels momentarily empowering when your heart is closing. You take all the uncertainty and discomfort and stress of the moment and project the blame for it onto the nearest person.

"Why," someone once asked me at a retreat I was hosting, "do we treat the people we most care about the worst?"

My wife, who was cofacilitating with me, answered, "Because they're around." If you've ever been on the receiving end of this, you probably know how much it feels like injustice.

Sometimes, it's an *actual* injustice.

Imagine you were convicted of a crime you regretted even as you were committing it, and now you're finally eligible for parole. They transport you to the courthouse, the judge calls your name, and you get to your feet as your thoughts race. How will the judge make the decision? Your crime was a relatively minor one. You've been locked up for years. You've taken responsibility for it. And you've been recognized for exemplary behavior behind bars. Surely, all of these factors will work in your favor, right?

There's only one problem: Your case is being called right before lunch.

In a 2011 study conducted at the University of Ben Gurion in Israel and Columbia University in New York City, scientists cataloged more than a thousand parole rulings made in 2009 by eight different judges. They found the likelihood of being paroled was approximately 65 percent at the beginning of the day, dropped to almost zero as the lunch hour approached, returned to 65 percent right after lunch, and dropped again for the rest of the afternoon.[1]

Judges are forgiving when they're full, and they're harsh when they're hungry.

The only other factors to influence their leniency were the number of previous incarcerations and the completion of a formal rehabilitation program. *Nothing else mattered.* It seems judges transfer the inner discomfort of their body into a strong outward opinion of the person in front of them. Our fixation on the outward-who over the inner-what is so complete that, even in a trained judge's eyes, a growling stomach creates an unsafe felon.

My wife didn't stand a chance with that missing veggie burger.

The Thirty-Thousand-Foot View

I was on a flight from Chicago to Phoenix recently, gazing out the window upon the vast plains of the American Midwest, when the pilot came onto the intercom and announced that we'd reached our cruising altitude of thirty-some-thousand feet. With my clients, I've often used the phrase "Let's take the thirty-thousand-foot view," but I'd never thought twice about where that phrase originated. The thirty-thousand-foot view is the panoramic, all-inclusive perspective you have of the land when you're flying way above it in an airplane. From that altitude, you can perceive patterns below—the patchwork of plowed fields, the way a river meanders, the cloverleaf of a highway interchange—that you'd never be able to see while on the ground in the midst of them. There are two ways to take a thirty-thousand-foot view of your triggered moments: seeing that you have the same reaction across very different situations, and seeing that you have very different reactions across very similar situations.

Same Reaction, Different Situations

I'm staring down at my plate, pushing the potato salad around with a fork, my head spinning with the effort to keep my mouth shut.

Years ago, on that Father's Day with the backward bagel, I didn't know enough to watch the inner-what instead of the outward-who. I just lashed out. Now, I know it's more about what's going on inside of me than who's standing in front of me, but what exactly is going on inside of me? Am I just hungry, like those eight judges in 2009? Or is there more going on here than meets the eye?

My kids' reaction suggests there's more going on here than meets the eye.

They're frozen, waiting to see what I'll do. They intuitively know there's a congruity between the reaction that is building in this situation and other situations in which I've blown my stack. My oldest may remember that errant Father's Day bagel. They all remember the morning I was playfully impersonating the television character Ted Lasso by staying wildly positive and optimistic, only to lose it when I discovered my wife had bought the wrong beans for the chili I was making. They probably also remember how I acted angry and aggrieved for most of her first Ironman training. In each of those very different situations, I responded almost identically.

Same reaction, different situations.

Your thirty-thousand-foot view can begin by noticing any congruity in your reaction across different situations and different people. Same reaction to your wife and your mom? Same reaction to your best friend and your kid? Same reaction to someone at work and someone on social media? Same reaction when your teenager wears your shirt without asking and when someone takes your parking spot at the supermarket? Or maybe it's the same reaction when the exact same someone does very different things, like forgetting your veggie burger and training for a triathlon. If it appears you may be the common denominator across a diverse range of people and provocations, it's possible you are.

I suppose that could sound like bad news, but it's actually the best news. After all, it's terribly complicated to solve countless separate conflicts with a dozen different people. It's much simpler to solve all of that conflict at once by discovering the source of it within yourself.

Different Reactions, Similar Situations

As I stand there pushing potato salad around my plate, my kids aren't running for cover yet, because I don't *always* respond that way. For every incident in which I've reacted dramatically to my wife, there's an almost identical incident in which I didn't. On any given night, I might shrug off this missing veggie burger, express thanks to her for everything else she's done, and gladly throw a patty on the grill myself. When she trained for her second Ironman, for instance, I had no problem with it. My kids are paused with their sodas halfway to their mouths because they're waiting to see which dad shows up tonight.

Different reactions, similar situations.

Your thirty-thousand-foot view can help you notice any incongruity in the nature or intensity of your reaction across similar situations. For instance, sometimes our reactions are proportionate to the provocation, but sometimes they are totally disproportionate. When your reactions seem erratic, you might want to stop acting out and start looking in.

"Yeah," a client once said to me, "but how many times do you have to touch the same hot stove before you can blame it for burning you?"

I knew he was talking about his business partner and the lack of acknowledgment he felt in that relationship.

"Good metaphor," I said. "Let's extend it. You don't feel a burn every time you touch the stove when it's set to that temperature—some days his indifference doesn't bother you at all. Different reactions, same situation. And sometimes you touch other stoves set to much lower temperatures and feel just as burned, like when your wife doesn't seem to appreciate the hotel you're staying in. Same reaction, different situations. Is it possible, given those congruities and incongruities, that the stove may not be *entirely* at fault here?"

He nodded, opening. "Okay, so what's causing the burn?"

"It's a great question, but you can't know the why until you've quit fixating on the who and started watching the what. Until you've become intimately familiar with the burn, if you will. What do you feel when you touch the stove?" I asked. I hooked air quotes around *the stove* and he knew I was talking about his business partner.

I watched him go inward. Good. The direction of his attention had pivoted. He was taking the thirty-thousand-foot view, and, sure enough, he saw something way down there in the vast plains of himself.

"I feel unappreciated," he said slowly. "Unneeded." He paused. "Huh. I feel unloved."

He had just exercised what I call the Pain Before People Principle: **If you can elevate your perspective, you'll see the patterns in your pain instead of the problems with your people.** He had simplified the solution to his triggered moments.

"Well done," I said. "You've just identified your intervening variable."

Identify Your Intervening Variable

One of the first things you learn in undergrad statistics is that correlation does not equal causation—just because two things happen around the same time doesn't mean one of them causes the other. For instance, when it's cold outside, people tend to wear winter coats, but the cold doesn't cause winter coats. Factories make those.

Later in your training, a new concept gets added to your statistical repertoire: the concept of mediating variables, also known as intervening variables. An intervening variable is the thing that *actually* explains the connection between the other two variables. In other words, when A and B coincide, sometimes it's actually because A triggers C, which triggers B. C is the intervening variable. Cold weather triggers physical discomfort, which leads to people donning winter coats. Physical discomfort is the intervening variable. Look closely and you'll see intervening variables everywhere:

- When an office has a pizza party, productivity tends to go up, but pizza doesn't cause greater productivity. Pizza parties lead to more team spirit, which results in more productivity. Team spirit is the intervening variable.
- Exercising vigorously appears to result in a better mood. In reality, strenuous exercise triggers the production of

endorphins, which results in better mood. The level of endorphins is the intervening variable.

- Research shows that better sleep results in better test scores. However, without the improved concentration that results from better sleep, the test scores wouldn't change at all. Concentration is the intervening variable.

My client's business partner appeared to be the direct cause of his animosity. He wasn't. The feeling of being unappreciated, unwanted, and unloved triggered my client to close his heart to his business partner. His business partner was merely the messenger delivering that experience, and my client was in the habit of shooting the messenger.

"Wait a second," you might say. "Sometimes people do terrible things that trigger terrible feelings, and sometimes you do need to do something about the messenger." Agreed. If you're in an abusive situation, do something about it—an open heart with healthy boundaries has a zero-tolerance policy for abuse. If you're in any other kind of situation, however, take a moment to slow down and simplify the solution by looking inward rather than outward. Watch the what instead of the who and become familiar with your intervening variable.

Pay attention to your pain instead of your people.

Here we have an opportunity to pivot the great conversation of our lives. For many years, the conversation has been between you and another or many others. Between you and your parents at first, or your siblings, or a grandparent. Between you and your friends or your teachers. Between you and your lover, your spouse, your children, your boss, your coworkers or your employees, your realtor or your landlord. Between you and the countless other human lives you've brushed up against. All these conversations, in one way or another, have been rooted in your longing for familiarity. The deep desire to be well-known and to know another well.

From the beginning, we locate the great conversation between us and everyone else because we are so dependent as human creatures upon the tribe for our safety. Across all mammalian species, the average age of maturity is a matter of months—just a few months of vulnerability and dependency before the creature is strong enough to defend itself and reproduce itself. Human beings are the exception. We exist in that state of dependency for years—therefore, being well-known is a matter of survival. "To the child, abandonment . . . is the equivalent of death," writes psychiatrist and bestselling author M. Scott Peck.[2] The only other terrestrial mammal that comes even close to us in this regard is the elephant. It should come as no surprise, then, that elephants also live in tribes, and they are among the only other mammals that clearly grieve.

We prioritize conversation with others because our familiarity to others is an existential necessity.

When you wander off, it's important that someone be thinking of you, concerned about you, so familiar with you that they'll know where to come looking for you, and so fond of you that they'll be willing to save you from whatever danger you might have wandered into. This is one reason loneliness feels so threatening to human beings. It's a pause in the conversation between us and the other. It gives space for decay of the familiarity you've worked so hard to establish, or it may feel like a failure to establish that familiarity in the first place. "For who can bear to feel himself forgotten?" writes the poet W. H. Auden.[3] When we human beings are lonely, we're not just having FOMO—our nervous system is scared for our lives.

Almost two decades after the mistaken bagel, it's still so tempting to make the forgotten burger a conversation between my wife and me. On this Fourth of July evening, though, it doesn't take long for me to make the pivot and simplify the solution. First, I get calm. I become aware of the fight-or-flight feeling in my chest—steel doors and warning sirens. I notice all my defenses demanding to be done—a tirade about the care I deserve, a lecture about her lack of organization. I breathe some margin around the chaos in my chest—the sirens quiet, the doors ease open a little. Through the doors, I can see a pain point that's become quite familiar to me in my yearslong conversation with it. It can be summed up in a word.

Unimportant.

The word has evolved over the years as I've gotten to know the pain point better. Someone recently told me the word for their pain point is *rejected*, and they wondered if it was accurate. I told them it wasn't up to me to decide. The conversation they have with their pain point over time will help them become more familiar with it. Their word for it may become even clearer, or they may discover *rejected* was the best way to describe it from the beginning.

The key is not to be correct about your pain point but to be in conversation with it.

Unimportant. It's the pain I feel when there's a missing veggie burger or a mistaken bagel. It's what I felt when there was a can of garbanzo beans instead of black beans in the pantry and when I was home alone with the kids for hours on a Sunday afternoon while my wife was out training for a triathlon.

Standing there in the kitchen, I hold a conversation with my pain. I can see that I'm reacting to *it*, not her. I tend to blame her for causing this pain, but I didn't even know she existed when this pain began in my life. I was already carrying this pain when we met, though I barely knew it. It's the pain that evaporated temporarily in her presence, and I called that evaporation falling in love. It's the pain I hoped our marriage would keep at bay for the rest of my life. Most of the time it does. When it doesn't, though, my heart has historically closed to it, and it has wreaked havoc on our family.

I look up from the potato salad and smile at her.

"You know how I need an illustration for the next chapter I'm writing?" I ask.

She nods.

"Well, I think I just found it."

She smiles too.

The kids, I'm told, smile as well, before taking a long swig of their sodas and going on with their night.

Exercise: The Two Hands Technique

Henry joins the call first.

This isn't unusual. He prides himself on being prompt. Sarah is usually transitioning from one domestic obligation or another and running a few seconds behind. It's an annoyance to Henry, and it's typically written all over his face. This time, though, a very different Henry appears on my screen. Disheveled hair. Pallid skin. Unshaven jaw. Bags beneath bloodshot eyes. His audio takes a minute to connect, and when it finally does, Sarah still hasn't appeared.

"Sarah's on the way?" I ask.

He sighs. "No, just me today." Something in him sounds . . . broken.

"Want to tell me about it?"

"Sure," he says, pausing and searching. "This is going to sound worse than it is, but . . . well, I pushed Owen." Before he drops his eyes from the screen, I see emotion in them I've never seen there before. "No," he continues, his voice cracking, "it's as bad as it sounds. I mean, I didn't hurt him badly or anything, but I definitely lost control, and he . . . he's been looking at me differently. Like he's scared of me." A longer pause, and then a more familiar look returns to his eyes. "It's crazy! My whole life is about protecting him, and now he's afraid of me. One little mistake and it erases everything. It's not fair!"

I let that hang in the air for a few moments before I ask, "Did you feel your heart open a little and then close quickly just now?"

His head falls into his hands. "Yeah. I did. I can't seem to control it, Doc. I'll be doing great, and then all of a sudden it closes out of nowhere."

"I hear you, man. I've been there. You can't control the closing, though."

"What *do* I do, then?" he asks, raising his eyes. He sounds sincere, and desperate.

"Instead of trying to control it, you can be in conversation with it. Before we get to that, though, tell me about Sarah. Why didn't she join us today?"

A long sigh. "She says this is proof she's not the only problem in our relationship. That I react this way to lots of people, and now I did it to our son. She says I need to deal with it before I do permanent damage to my relationship with him. She said if she was here, I'd just focus on her, and I need to focus on myself."

Sarah's a wise woman.

"Want to tell me what happened with Owen?"

His head falls back into his hands. "We were on a hike. An epic hike. Just the two of us. We'd been planning it all year. We were halfway to the peak and stopped for lunch, and he told me about some kids who've been bullying him at school. He started to get real down on himself. Like depressed. I was just trying to pep him up, you know? I explained to him that what you focus on expands. I told him he just needed to practice some gratitude for the friends he does have. Focus on the present. Like, look around, we're on this amazing hike, let's just enjoy what we have right now." He sighs. "Anyway, the more I tried to pep him up, the more down he got, just like Sarah. He said he didn't want to hike anymore. I acted like I was gonna go on without him, but he wouldn't budge. I raised my voice,

I think, and he started to cry. I threatened to ground him from his devices if he didn't cut it out, and that just made him cry harder. It drove me crazy, and I . . ." He trails off.

"Go ahead."

"I lifted him by the armpits and pushed him up the hill. He fell down and went totally nuclear. So I just gave up. We walked back to the car and drove home in silence. It was terrible."

"And you see parallels to how you react with Sarah?" I ask.

"It's almost identical," he concedes, sounding utterly defeated.

"Two totally different people and different relationships, but the same reaction happening within you," I clarify.

He shakes his head as if to deny it, but his words say something else. "Yeah, and it happens with my team too." He points at the Hilltop Investments logo embroidered on his shirt. "Though I never lose my cool with them. Well, *rarely*."

"Anyone else?"

He pauses to consider this before answering.

"Sure. Pretty much anyone who's unnecessarily negative."

"Let's start there, then," I say. "You spend a lot of time in closed-hearted conversation with the negative people around you. What if instead you simplified your approach by conversing with the experience you have inside of you when the people around you are, as you call it, negative?"

"Not sure what that looks like," he says, sounding exceptionally skeptical. "Got a conversation starter for me?"

"Sure," I say. "I call it the two hands technique. Want to try it?" He shrugs assent.

"Okay, go ahead and close your eyes. Visualize yourself back in that scene with Owen during the hike. He's telling you about the bullies at school, and you're feeling your heart start to close. You watch your impulse to sell him happiness and mentor him toward gratitude. You don't wield it. Instead, you regulate your nervous system until your reaction feels more like a response. Let me know when you're there."

A few moments pass. I can see his eyeballs darting back and forth beneath his closed eyelids.

"All right, I'm there," he says.

"Good. Now, hold your left hand out in front of you at arm's length, closed in a fist." He does so. "At the same time, hold your right hand out in front of you at arm's length, open, palm facing outward, like a stop sign." He does that too.

"Your hands right now represent the two things your closed heart is always doing. It is always either clinging to an experience it wants to have—attaching to it, trying to hold on to it. Or it's resisting another experience it doesn't want to have—pushing it away, trying to stop it from happening. Make sense?" He nods.

"Okay, let's converse with that closed fist first. What are you holding on to in this moment with Owen? What is the experience you want to have that you don't want to let go of?"

"That's an easy one," he says, his eyes still closed. "I've been imagining this hike since we planned it last winter. I wanted it to be an epic father-son experience. Pure joy. A great memory for both of us."

"Good," I say. "Anything else? Anything that feels perhaps a little more tender?"

After a moment, Henry's chin starts to tremble ever so slightly. "Yeah," he says, "I want us to feel close. Real close, you know? Like a bond that can never be broken."

I let him sit with that for another moment. "Okay, now let's converse with that stop sign you're holding out. What is the experience you are pushing away in this moment?"

This one is a little more difficult for him. He takes some time to reflect before he speaks. "I don't want him to be all defeatist and mopey and weak. That kind of crap just drives me crazy. Where does it get you? Feeling depressed and terrible about yourself, that's where. I can't stand people who do that."

"Whoa, those are strong words. *Weak. Mopey. Defeatist.* I can see why you wouldn't be eager to experience them. Now I want you to try one more thing. On the count of three, take a deep breath, and on the slow out-breath, spread your arms wide and imagine those experiences passing into you and through you, like there's an open window in the center of you, and they are a breeze you can feel moving through it. Go ahead now. Deep breath, release it, arms open, and imagine *weak*, *mopey*, and *defeatist* passing right through you."

He breathes deeply and exhales, but then with his arms about halfway open, he shakes his head emphatically. "Nope," he says. "Not doing it. What's the point? Where will that get me?"

It never gets old, watching a heart discover what it's currently unwilling to open to.

"I'm going to pretend that question isn't rhetorical, Henry. You see, **you think you're passing through life, but you're not; life is passing through you.** Except it can't get through you. You're like a sieve, deciding which experiences are worth having and which aren't. The problem is, the ones you don't want to have don't pass through, they get caught in you like little irritating pebbles. And pebbles add up. There is a great weight to the experiences that have gotten caught in us. And the more of them there are, the fuller the sieve gets, and the harder it is for anything to get through."

His shoulders are slumped again—Henry's way of showing he's receiving something that's hard to receive.

"You can't force yourself to stay open," I continue. "Instead, you can gradually pivot from being a sieve to being a window. To do that, you have to stay in conversation with the experiences you don't want to have. Would you be willing to commit to that singular focus?"

"Yeah," he agrees, "I can do that."

And with that, Henry has crossed the threshold into the second part of the Peaceful Pivot Process: getting free of the emotional patterns that underpin his triggered moments.

5

Trace Your Triggers Through Time

> Where we cannot go in our mind, our memory, or our body is where we cannot be straight with another, with the world, or with our self.
>
> David Whyte

Halloween is still a week away, but the season's first snowflakes are already falling as my kids and I work together in our driveway.

There's a cord of split firewood piled in front of our garage, wider than the garage door itself and taller than tweenager Caitlin. It'll last us all winter. Our job is to stack it in the garage before dark. It's an annual ritual that always concludes with some hot cocoa.

The kids work hard until all that's left in the driveway is a mess of sloughed off bark and dirt. They ask if they can call it quitting time and head in for cocoa. I'm genuinely grateful for their effort and give them the green light to go inside.

In the gloaming, I get out a shovel and begin scooping up the leftovers. It's easy labor. The late autumn colors of the forest we live in deepen as the light goes out of the day. The snow falls silently. A streetlamp comes on in a clearing up the road—it's how I picture the lamppost in Narnia where Lucy met Tumnus. My heart is as open as an eight-lane highway at two in the morning.

Until I look up at the kitchen windows.

My family is framed there in the warm, honey hues of the home, which stand in stark contrast to the dark blue dusk descending out here in the cold. *Must be nice*, I think, before returning to my toil. Scoop, scoop goes the shovel. *Why am I out here all by myself?* goes my mind. The answer is obvious: A few minutes ago, I gladly told my kids they could go inside. Nevertheless, something fiery is flaring up within me. Scoop, scoop goes the shovel again. *It's not fair!* goes my mind again. I can hear the petulance in the protest. The childishness of it. It's clear my heart is quickly and inexplicably closing around my pain point. I'm feeling unimportant, neglected, and abandoned. Despite my ongoing conversation with it, my pain point persists.

What's wrong *with me?* I wonder.

This question has some close cousins like "Why can't I just get over this?" and "When am I finally going to grow up?" These are frustrating questions, but they are also common questions at this point in the Peaceful Pivot Process. You've taken up the conversation with your pain point, and it's produced some quick successes at staying calmly openhearted in your most triggered moments. You may even have experienced a moment of zen here and there. However, staying calm is still a bit of a crapshoot—sometimes you can pull it off, sometimes you can't. Consequently, now you're not just triggered, you're *erratically* triggered, and your unpredictable behavior is giving your people hives. This is no way to live.

You feel stuck, so you're more willing than ever to hear any idea that might help.

In other words, you're like the hero at the midpoint of the hero's journey.

This Is Your Hero's Journey

In 1949, a little-known professor of literature at Sarah Lawrence College in Yonkers, New York, published a book that has had more influence on storytelling and screenwriting than anything else ever written. Joseph Campbell's *The Hero with a Thousand Faces* identified a pattern found in the stories of cultures throughout human history, and he argued that our most powerful stories always follow this pattern. Campbell called it the hero's journey, and he observed that the hero's deepest transformation always happens at the very midpoint of the journey.

Students of Campbell's work have described this midpoint transformation as a pivot from the hero's A-story to their B-story.[1] The A-story is what the hero is focused on at the beginning of the tale. In the A-story, the hero can't see the big picture yet, so they're trying to solve relatively superficial problems in overly simplistic ways. This isn't bad; it's just incomplete. The A-story is what gets the hero going, but clinging to it is what ultimately keeps them stuck.

What compels us to start our transformation often keeps us from completing our transformation.

In the B-story, by contrast, the hero finally faces a deeper problem. If the hero doesn't transition to this B-story, the journey feels disappointingly anticlimactic, whereas if they throw themselves into the B-story, it might very well feel like an epic tale. Take the original *Star Wars* trilogy, for instance. The first installment of the saga, *A New Hope*, was released in 1977. It has outdated special effects, a pacing that should rankle modern audiences, and dialogue cheesier than a Chicago-style deep dish pizza, yet generation after generation continues to fall in love with it. Why? Because George Lucas read *The Hero with a Thousand Faces* after conceiving the trilogy, and he revised the story to match the hero's journey.

Consequently, the trilogy nails the midpoint moment for its hero, Luke Skywalker.

Near the beginning of the first film, we meet Luke, who's working as a farmhand for his aunt and uncle and longing to trade the tedium of his provincial existence for a life up in the stars. In other words, he wants to solve his A-story problem—boredom—with an A-story solution: adventure. However, an early scene portends the deeper problem Luke will have to face. Over a meal, Luke expresses a wish to know more about his father, and his uncle commands him to forget about it. Luke's past is his B-story.

He just doesn't know it yet.

Driven by his A-story ambitions, Luke discovers his neighbor Obi-Wan "Ben" Kenobi was part of an old galactic rebellion. After a dark turn of events, Luke leaves his planet with Ben and gets embroiled in a renewed rebellion against the evil Empire, becoming a key figure in that rebellion by the end of the first movie. His A-story problem has been solved. He's found an epic adventure. Then, in *The Empire Strikes Back*—the middle movie of the trilogy—Luke experiences his midpoint moment. At the end of an iconic light saber duel with Darth Vader, the galaxy's villain, Luke finally finds out more about his father.

"Obi-Wan never told you what happened to your father," says Vader.

"He told me enough. He told me you killed him," Luke spits back at him.

"No," Vader replies, "*I* am your father."[2]

The rest of the trilogy—Luke's B-story—will revolve around Luke's realization of, and reckoning with, his past. While there are, of course, other layers to Luke's story, this dimension of it highlights the key differences between a hero's A-story and B-story. The A-story is about the hero getting what they want; the B-story is about the hero getting what they need. The A-story is about self-satisfaction; the B-story is about self-transformation. "Forget the past," Luke's uncle had commanded him. That's A-story thinking. In the B-story of a hero's journey, you don't forget your past, you face it.

The Peaceful Pivot Process is no different.

A Better Question

I stand in the driveway, the lighted windows of the home glowing warmer and brighter as the evening outside turns from blue to black ink. My wife is wearing an oven mitt as she tips the contents of a steaming pot into a big, brown mug. She says something and my daughter laughs in the way that always brings tears to her eyes. I adore it, and her, and all of them. It makes me want to go inside and break things.

"What's *wrong* with me?" I ask again, this time aloud.

Hearing those words echo back to me in the empty night, I'm reminded of a book that was published just a few months earlier. In it, the authors—psychiatrist Bruce Perry and self-transformation phenom Oprah Winfrey—make the case that when you find yourself inexplicably triggered by something in the present, your reaction probably isn't primarily about the present. It's about the past. The problem is, the part of your brain tasked with handling threats can't tell time, so it can't distinguish between past and present. Therefore, they suggest that when you are tempted to ask what's wrong with you, you should try asking a slightly but dramatically different question:

What *happened* to you?

In his conversation with Oprah, Dr. Perry tells of the first time he explained the timelessness of painful experience to a

Korean War veteran named Mike, who'd been triggered by a motorcycle backfiring. Dr. Perry began by taking a sheet of paper and drawing an upside-down triangle with three horizontal lines dividing it into four parts, explaining that the brain is like a layer cake, with the cortex—the part of our brain that makes us uniquely human—at the top. He continued,

> This is the part of the brain that can "tell time." When the cortex is "online" and active, we can think about the past and look forward to the future. We know which things are in our past and which things are present.
>
> Now look at the bottom of the brain—the brainstem. . . . There are no networks in the bottom part of the brain that think or tell time. Sometimes we refer to this part of the brain as the reptilian brain, so think of what a lizard can do—they don't plan much, or think; they mostly live in the moment and react. But we humans, thanks to the top part of our brain—the cortex—can invent, create, plan, and tell time.
>
> Input from all of our senses—vision, hearing, touch, smell, taste—first comes into our brain in the lower areas. None of our sensory input goes directly to the cortex; everything first connects to the lower part of the brain. Once the signal comes into the brainstem, it is processed. Basically, the incoming signal is matched against previously stored experiences. In this case, the matching process connected the motorcycle backfire with gunfire. . . . And since your brainstem can't tell time, or know that many years have passed, it activates the stress response and you have a full-blown threat response. . . . Your brainstem can't say, "Hey don't get so stirred up, Korea was thirty years ago. That sound was simply a motorcycle backfiring."[3]

He went on to explain to Mike that when the present experience finally reaches the cortex—where it might be differentiated from the past—the cortex is often already deactivated by the stress response, and for good reason. If a few thousand years ago you were confronted by a predator and your cortex stayed active—comparing this predator to other predators you've faced—you didn't survive. Cortexes that took the time to differentiate past and present under threat weren't passed on in the gene pool. Thanks to your ancestors, when the present in any way resembles a particularly painful part of your past, time ceases to exist in your brain and body.

It's all happening now.

Of course, your present closing is always at least a little bit about the present moment. It's a little bit about the fact that your friend forgot your birthday and your teenager won't come out of their bedroom and your toddler threw a temper tantrum right in front of your new pastor and your boss can't find a single good thing to say about your hard work and your spouse is inexplicably moody. Yes, your closing is always a little bit about what's happening right now. However, without the past pushing its way into the present through your loud lower brain and your quiet cortex, you'd have much less trouble keeping your heart open to what is.

From my vantage point in the driveway, I can't see the hot cocoa mustaches on my kids, but I can imagine them. I can also imagine how confused and hurt they'd be if I stormed into the house right now and hollered at them for not being out there in the driveway helping me. Instead, I think of that other question.

What *happened* to me?

Transform Your Triggers into a Bull's-Eye

"The past is never dead," wrote the great American novelist William Faulkner. "It's not even past."[4]

For many of us, that can be shocking—as shocking as discovering Darth Vader is your father and you have to fight him again with a laser sword to save the galaxy. However, everywhere we look, there's evidence of the past in the present. For instance, imagine you're standing on the shore of a placid pond and suddenly you spot a hundred circular ripples moving outward from some unseen center. Would you start wondering about the hundreds of things that happened to the pond to produce a hundred different ripples? Would you look only at the largest, most recent ripple in order to fully understand the reason for its existence? Would you search the whole pond for the point of origin of the ripples, with no idea where to really begin?

Of course not.

Rather, you'd intuitively know a few things about what's happening here. You'd know the most recent ripple is not distinct from the past but is intimately connected to it—a direct result of the ripples that preceded it. You'd also know the concentric circles created by the ripples are forming a bull's-eye around the originating event. Furthermore, you'd know something plunked the pond in the center of the bull's-eye. Finally, you'd probably wonder what the something was.

The error we make when we first ask, "What happened to me?" is to go in search of early memories. This can be just as frustrating as asking, "What's wrong with me?" We understand very little about how memories are made, stored, and retrieved. What we do know is that *trying* to remember something, or *needing* to remember something, often pushes a memory further into the depths. In other words, when you're triggered and experience another ripple in your pond, it's best not to do a deep dive to retrieve some pebble of explanation from the muddy floor of your memory. Rather, you can stay here on the surface where your triggers are and simply follow those ripples one by one back to the center.

You can trace your triggers through time.

Consider Mike, the Korean War vet who Dr. Perry taught about the timelessness of past pain. Let's assume for a moment that Mike has amnesia for his deployment in the war. However, when a motorcycle backfires, he's triggered and feels like his life is in danger. That's a ripple. It reminds him of the time a firecracker went off and startled him. That's an earlier ripple. The firecracker reminded him of the time his wife slammed a cupboard door. Ripple. And that reminded him of their grandson dropping a metal firetruck on the ceramic tile. Ripple. Mike doesn't have to remember anything about Korea to follow the ripples of his triggers back through time in the direction of their origin—his pond was clearly plunked at some point in the past by an experience that included explosive sounds and a fear of being harmed. Now Mike is in a conversation with his pain *and* his past, and he has crossed into his B-story.

"I can see where you're going with this," a skeptical client once said to me, "but my parents did the best they could, and besides, they're not gonna change anyway."

"Of course they did, and of course they aren't," I replied. "This isn't about them. This is about you and about your pain point rippling out across time. Would you insist the ripples in a pond didn't start with the plunk of a pebble simply because the people who threw the pebbles were good people, or they threw them with the best of intentions, or they'll never stop throwing pebbles?" He shook his head reluctantly.

"The nature of the thrower has no bearing upon the physics of the pebble and its impact upon the pond, nor on the pain point that's been rippling outward ever since, getting bigger and bigger with each successive closing."

A long silence hung between us. I waited. Finally, he spoke. "Okay, so how do I get started? You know I don't have many memories from my childhood."

"That's okay," I said. "We're not searching for a specific memory anyway. We're interested in the ripple of pain that runs through many of your memories, possibly with many different people, not just the ones who raised you. We don't need to go in search of the past, because the past is always pushing its way into the present, precisely at the moment your heart closes. That's how you transform your triggers. You see them differently."

Your triggers aren't a present you have to fix, they're a past you get to face.

From Trigger to Turning Point

I close my eyes in the dark solitude of the driveway. Instead of asking a question—"What happened to you?"—I do a sentence completion task: "This wouldn't be so hard if it didn't remind me of . . ."

Sometimes the completion of that sentence comes easily, sometimes slowly. Sometimes the answer comes clearly, sometimes vaguely. It might be a memory of something that happened the day before or a decade before. Like Mike the Korean War vet, you might be able to repeat the prompt several times and remember ripple after ripple, tracing your triggers further and further back in time, until you sense you're close to the epicenter of your pain point.

In this case, I can complete the sentence almost immediately, with a memory I haven't thought about since the night it happened more than thirty years ago. "This wouldn't be so hard if it didn't remind me of . . ." I say aloud into the silence, "that Sunday night in the driveway." And just like that, my trigger turns into a time machine.

It's a wintery night in my adolescence. Was it really a Sunday night? I'm not sure, but I'm pretty sure I had school the next day. Did it happen more than once? Again, I'm not sure. What I clearly remember is this: I'm outside on my own after dark doing my winter chore—shoveling the driveway until it's clear. The driveway is forty yards long and ten yards wide at its greatest girth. That's fine. Even at thirteen I can outwork a driveway. What I can't outwork is the wind. Every time I clear a section, the wind blows drifting snow over it, erasing what I've just accomplished.

Finally, I pause, my fingers painfully cold and my hair wet with sweat beneath my stocking cap. I look up and down the empty street and then at the warmly lit windows of my house, and I howl with the loneliness of it.

"It's not fair!" I scream aloud, my little protest easily drowned out by Mother Nature's power.

"How are we healed of our wounding memories?" asks Henri J. M. Nouwen. "We are healed first of all by letting them be available, by leading them out of the corner of forgetfulness, and by remembering them as part of our life stories. What is forgotten is unavailable and what is unavailable cannot be healed."[5]

More than thirty years later, I let that howl of loneliness become available. I lead it out of the corner of forgetfulness. I welcome it back into the kinship of memory. Standing there in the driveway, I know there's nothing wrong with me; there are just things that have *happened* to me. I'm a ripple of loneliness, made by a ripple of loneliness, made by a ripple of loneliness. Are there more ripples for me to remember? For sure. Do I need to remember them all tonight? Not at all.

My cortex is back online again.

I'm in my B-story now, facing what happened to me. I can tell the difference between past and present once more. And that's just enough perspective to open my heart to what is happening here and now. I look through the kitchen window again, grateful for my kids' help in the driveway, aware I can go inside and join them whenever I want and am eager to do so.

Not only is the moment of your closing about more than the person in front of you, it's also about more than the *present* in front of you. As Oprah says in that conversation with Dr. Perry, "If we want to understand the oak, it's back to the acorn we must go."[6] You can transform your triggers into your turning point.

By learning how to tell time again.

Exercise: Remember Your Ripples

"I see it everywhere," says Henry.

He looks like neither the carefully-coiffed businessman I met at the beginning of our work together nor the shell of himself that appeared on my screen two months ago. In the weeks after the incident with his son, he has fully dedicated himself to seeing the emotional patterns that underpin his triggered moments. At one point, Sarah offered to join him for a session again, and he declined, saying he wanted to stay focused on his own inner work.

"I really can't stand negativity in any form," he told me a month ago after carefully observing the same closing of his heart across different situations. "I close down immediately. Sometimes it's subtle, sometimes it's not. What's crazy is, my highest value is freedom."

"Why is that crazy?" I asked.

"Because I've always believed freedom is happiness, but they're not the same thing. If I insist on positivity," he hooked air quotes around that last word, "I'm actually not free to experience the rest of my life. It's like I've built a big wall around my happiness, and I've told everybody they can't join me in there unless they're going to be happy too. So, I'm free inside the walls of my little life, but that's where the freedom ends. I'm not free to roam. I can't connect with Sarah when she's overwhelmed. I can't connect with Owen when he feels hurt. I couldn't connect with my friend Jay last week when he told me his mom was diagnosed with Alzheimer's. And that's no freedom at all."

After that call, we spent several sessions identifying the pain point that gets triggered in him when others are anything but happy. It was slow going at first, but the more he was able to linger with that burning feeling in his chest, the more he realized it was accompanied by a "dark" feeling in his gut. He stayed in conversation with that, becoming more familiar with the somatic and cognitive "fingerprints" of that experience so he could bring more attention to it as it ebbed and flowed during his daily life. Now, he has appeared on my screen with his edges as soft as I've ever seen them, saying he can see the dark feeling everywhere.

"Tell me more," I say.

"Just yesterday I was on a walk with Sarah. We were having a great time. Holding hands. Really connecting, you know?"

I nod.

"Then she starts talking about how she's been trying to teach Grace the alphabet, to get her ready for kindergarten, and she's worried Grace is picking it up too slowly. Like she might have a learning disorder or something. And I can feel my heart start to close. So, I do everything we've talked about, and sure enough, there is the lead ball underneath the closing. I opened my heart to it, and all of a sudden I'm feeling this pressure at the back of my eyes. I just had to shut down for the rest of the walk." He shakes his head in bewilderment. "What is wrong with me?"

"You're doing great work," I reassure him, "but we need to change that question of yours ever so slightly. Instead of asking what's wrong with you, let's ask what happened to you. Are you ready to explore how that pain point can be found not just across people in your life at present but across time as well, going back into your past?" Some of his sharper edges suddenly return.

"Doc, I told you I don't do the past."

"I hear you," I say, "and I have no interest in dragging your past into the present. I'm interested in the parts of your past that keep pushing their way into the present in the form of your closing heart. Would you be willing to follow the trail of your triggers as far back as you can go today? No pressure to find anything or feel anything. Just allowing whatever comes to mind. What do you say, want to give it a try?"

There's silence, then a sigh. "Sure," he agrees, but it's clear we're well outside his happiness walls.

"Great. We can call this off whenever you want to, okay?" He rubs at a temple and nods.

"Okay. It's just a little sentence completion game I call Remember Your Ripples." I spare him the metaphor, and he doesn't ask. "I'm going to give you the same prompt over and over, and you're just going to do your best to respond."

He rolls his shoulders and tilts his head from side to side like he's warming up for a fight. I've come to appreciate this about him. He's the best kind of fighter.

"Let's start by reflecting on that episode with Sarah yesterday. Close your eyes and take a moment to place yourself back in that situation. When you feel like you're there, let me know." His eyes close and his breathing slows.

"Okay, I'm there," he says.

"Good, now complete this sentence: That wouldn't have been so hard if it didn't remind me of . . ."

He immediately scoffs. "Um, every other time in our relationship."

"Right," I say, laughing, "but let's get specific, and let's try to recall an event early in your relationship with Sarah."

"Like, say, the first day of our honeymoon?" Apparently, this isn't requiring much of a leap for him.

"Sure."

"One of my favorite things about Sarah when we were dating was how positive she was. Even on our wedding day, when it was raining and we had to move everything indoors, she was a trouper. Then we got to Cabo for our honeymoon, and we were at breakfast our first morning there. An oceanside patio. The sun was just up. The food was amazing. We had our whole lives in front of us, and she started wondering if it was too much to ask of her parents to carry all of our wedding gifts home."

He pauses, and when he speaks again the verb tense has changed. He's fully back in the scene.

"I try to reassure her and move on, but she just can't get past it. Then she starts worrying about whether or not she placed too much burden on her bridesmaids over the last few months. I keep telling her to forget about it and focus on the amazing food, but the more I tell her to move on, the more she tries to explain why it's on her mind. It was our first big fight. We gave each other the silent treatment by the pool all day. So much for wedded bliss, huh?"

"Great work," I say. "Now, complete this sentence: That wouldn't have been so hard if it hadn't reminded me of . . ."

This one is a little harder for him, and the silence is drawn out, until he barks a laugh. "I can say anything?"

"Yes. In fact, I want you to say whatever comes to mind first, without censoring yourself."

"All right. The first thing that came to mind was my first boss at the accounting firm where I worked right out of college. Amanda Barker. That woman couldn't be positive about a cupcake. Always focused on what was going wrong, not what was going right. Actually, she was probably my motivation to start a company of my own and lead it by focusing on the positive. Amanda Barker. I owe my success to her."

I don't give him a beat to collect his thoughts.

"Amanda Barker wouldn't have been so hard if she hadn't reminded me of . . ."

The pause is even longer this time. When he speaks, the bravado is gone, replaced by caution.

"My high school girlfriend comes to mind. Wendy Waters. Great name for her, because she sure went in waves. We'd be great for months at a time, then she'd go dark on me for weeks. I was always trying to pull her out of it, but she was a lost cause.

Dated her for three years of high school and one of college before I met Sarah. Four wasted years."

"Wendy Waters wouldn't have been so hard if she hadn't reminded me of . . ."

The answer comes more quickly than I expected. "My grandma. What a wet blanket. I hated going to her house. She'd watch us on weekends. You couldn't touch anything around there. Everything you did was a problem."

Pause. His eyes are still closed but I can see them moving back and forth rapidly beneath his eyelids as he continues.

"Meals there were miserable. She'd complain the entire time. About my grandpa. About her friends. About her life. I just tuned out and traced patterns on the tablecloth with my eyes."

"Was that your mom's mom, or your dad's?"

"Mom's," he says, his jaw clenching.

"Grandma wouldn't have been so hard if she hadn't reminded me of . . ."

There is a long, long pause, before he smiles the angriest smile I've ever seen.

"Did I ever tell you my mom was in a psychiatric hospital when I was in the third grade?"

6

Feel Your Way to Freedom

> The quickest way for anyone to reach the sun and the light of day is not to run west, chasing after the setting sun, but to head east, plunging into the darkness until one comes to the sunrise.
>
> Gerald Sittser

It's the morning of my birthday, and I'm lying on my bathroom floor, wrapped in a towel, my legs propped at a ninety-degree angle on the toilet seat. I cannot move.

Thirty minutes ago, all was well, or so it seemed.

I'd woken to birthday cheer from my wife and kids and friends and social media. Even Starbucks remembered me. I'd cleared my morning so I could get a slow start and treat myself to a massage. The slow start had begun with a long, hot shower. My fingers were prunes by the time I reached for a towel and bent over to dry my legs.

When I tried to stand again, the celebration came to an end.

The pain in my back was obliterating, a thousand invisible knives punching into the base of my spine. I couldn't straighten up, let alone take a step, so I wrapped the towel around my waist, rolled onto the floor, and hoisted my legs onto the toilet seat—the one position that provides relief from lower back pain.

Unfortunately, this isn't my first rodeo.

Fifteen minutes later, I've air-dried, but the pain is still intensifying, and I'm reviewing the three things I know. First, my recurring back pain isn't a physical problem. Scans have confirmed I have a few aging discs, but nothing structural can explain so much pain triggered by movements as mild as getting out of a chair, picking up a paper clip, or drying my shins with a towel. Second, I know I'm experiencing muscle spasms triggered by emotional pain I've been blocking, and the spasms will relax once I feel the emotions.

Finally, I know a psychological theory about dying.

It originated in the 1960s, when Swiss American psychiatrist Elisabeth Kübler-Ross took umbrage with the way her terminally ill patients were shunned by the medical community as failures of medicine. She rebelled against the system by having deep conversations with them. Based on two hundred formal interviews of terminally ill people, she identified a common emotional pattern in the dying process. In 1969, she published *On Death and Dying*, in which she described the five stages of grief: denial, anger, bargaining, sadness*, and acceptance.[1]

Though the medical community initially greeted the book with skepticism, her model was so accurate—and therefore so helpful—that within a decade it became a cornerstone of the burgeoning hospice movement. Thirty years later, *Time*

*Kübler-Ross originally called this stage *depression*, though that term is now commonly used in reference to a severe mental health condition, not a normal experience in the grieving process. Therefore, the word *sadness* is used here for the sake of clarity.

magazine recognized her as one of the most important thinkers of the twentieth century, and in 2024, Simon & Schuster placed her book on a list among the one hundred most important of all time. It has stood the test of time not just because it shows us how to die.

It also shows us how to live and how to *feel*.

In her five stages, Kübler-Ross incorporated the four core human emotions—happiness (aka acceptance), anger, fear (aka bargaining), and sadness—as well as our human capacity to deny our emotions altogether. Essentially, she showed we have three ways of resisting our pain (denial, anger, and fear), a singular way of experiencing it (sadness), and the peace that comes with its passage (acceptance). Another way of saying it is that we have three ways of keeping our heart closed to our pain, one way of opening to it, and then finally the fruit of that opening:

Once you can keep your heart open to your deepest pain, you can keep your heart open to anything.

A Closed Heart: Denial, Anger, and Bargaining

The first three stages of grief reflect three different methods for avoiding our pain. Denial is the preference for fun over feeling it. Anger is the preference for fighting over feeling it. And bargaining is the preference for fixing it over feeling it.

Fun over feeling. Denial is the active—though usually unconscious—effort to suppress our emotions altogether, which makes it the most cleverly disguised way to dismiss our pain. Several of its most common disguises are distraction, dependence, and drivenness. In modern times, for instance, smartphone notifications, social media algorithms, and Netflix binges are popular ways to stay distracted. Dependence can take countless forms, including video games, gambling, sex, food, alcohol, drugs, pornography, and relational drama in its various forms. Finally, in modern America especially, drivenness is one of the most celebrated forms of emotional denialism. **We'd prefer to burn out rather than to let our emotions out.**

Lying there on the bathroom floor, it's clear that drivenness has been my preferred method of denial in recent months. I'd recently published a new book, and my calendar had been jammed with speaking events and travel. I'd been doing everything and feeling nothing for quite some time. Thanks to Kübler-Ross, though, I know anger is the most natural way to move out of my denial and into my emotions.

Fighting over feeling. Anger is an emotion, but it is not pain; rather, it's the desire to *inflict* pain. The purpose of anger is to keep you outwardly focused rather than inwardly feeling. Any sort of judgment, criticism, condemnation, and rage keeps you moving away from your center and the pain that resides there.

The day before my birthday, I'd come into information that proved the people I paid to assist me with my book launch had not helped but harmed the effort. I'd brushed it off and gotten back to work. Now, on the bathroom floor, I let myself think about it, and the anger begins to build. Unfortunately, though, when you're having back spasms, feeling anger is also excruciating. The adrenaline activates musculature, so the spasms intensify. My anger will have to give way to something else, and once again Kübler-Ross shows the way: The next step is bargaining.

Fixing over feeling. Bargaining comprises the constellation of ways your brain tries to solve your pain before you have to feel it. It's a way of staying in your head rather than descending into your heart. However, because thoughts are both endless and rapid, bargaining tends to be anxiety-ridden. Anxiety, while quite uncomfortable, is not actually pain either. Rather, it's the final negotiation with your pain. You are dancing around it until you are ready to dance with it.

Over on the bathroom sink, my phone is vibrating intermittently with more birthday wishes as I tune in to my mind and its bargaining. Should I confront the people who let me down? Was it my fault somehow? Should I repair the relationship or end it? The bargaining is more focused on my people than my publishing, which tells me that my pain is more relational than vocational. In fact, I'm recognizing some familiar ripples in it—ripples like *unimportant*, *neglected*, and *abandoned*. Now, according to Kübler-Ross, all I've got to do is open my heart to those ripples.

When it comes to opening our heart, pain isn't the problem, it's the path.

An Opening Heart: The Four Phases of Sadness

Some years ago, we woke up one morning after a torrential rain to discover our basement flooded. The sump pump had worked fine for years, but a piece of old construction debris had gotten lodged in its float switch—a little pillow on the side of the pump that rises with the water level until it triggers the pump to kick on. The morning of the flood, I discovered the debris, removed it, and the pump turned on, clearing the basement in a powerful torrent of rushing water. After that, the switch worked fine again, and the pump kicked on every time there was enough seepage to trigger it. The subsequent expulsions were always quieter and quicker than the huge one during the flood. A gentle gush instead of a fierce fire hose.

Sadness is like rainwater seeping into our soul, and to feel it fully we usually go through the same four phases as that sump pump.

Phase 1: Sadness when you start. Kids cry all the time. At first, they cry for feedings and burpings and diaper changes. Then they cry when they get hurt, when they need help, when they don't get what they want or when what they want is taken away, when they lose something or fail at something. Kids will cry for no reason at all except that they're sad, and sadness is reason enough. A kid's heart is open. What's in them flows out.

Eventually, though, most kids stop crying altogether.

There are a lot of ways to mark the dividing line between childhood and adulthood. I wonder if the day the tears stop is one of them. I wonder if that's what Jesus was talking about when he said, "Truly I tell you, unless you change and become like little children, you will never enter the kingdom of heaven" (Matt. 18:2–3). It's one of his most important teachings, yet he provides no additional instructions about how to become childlike again.

I wonder if he didn't tell us because he was *showing* us.

When his friend died, he took time to sob over him, resulting in the shortest verse in the Bible: "Jesus wept" (John 11:35). He looked out over the city of Jerusalem and sobbed over it as well. The book of Isaiah describes Jesus as a man "of suffering, and familiar with pain" (53:3). His most popular sermon begins with "blessed are the poor in spirit" and "blessed are those who mourn" (Matt. 5:3–4). Jesus did not suppress his sadness; he expressed his sadness.

When we were children, our emotional sump pump worked just fine for a while. Our tears weren't exceptions to the rule, they *were* the rule. At some point, though, our float switch got stuck.

Phase 2: Sadness when it's stuck. The debris that gets stuck on our float switch can take many forms. For instance, a parent may indirectly show you they can't handle your sadness, or they may tell you quite directly that sadness is for sissies. One client got emotional when he expressed a lifelong fear. He brushed at the tears in his eyes and declared, "I'm acting like a baby."

Where did he get the idea that sadness is immature and weak?

Maybe for you the pressure to stay dry-eyed came from all the other seemingly sadness-free kids in the fourth grade. Or the message that faith is supposed to make you happy, when actually it's just supposed to make you whole. Maybe you were pressured to put everyone else's emotions ahead of your own, lest you be "selfish." Sometimes we do it to ourselves simply because having fun is easier than having feelings. And sometimes, the pain of our childhood was just too much for us to bear—this is what we call *trauma*—so we placed our finger on the float switch and never lifted it again.

Another client was caught in a drug addiction by her husband, who had one foot out the door. She was getting lots of help and becoming aware of a great sadness she'd been carrying around since her parents' divorce when she was seven. She said the idea of feeling her sadness made her anxious. "Right here," she said, placing her hand over her chest, "I get really tight."

I nodded, then explained: Our sadness begins in our gut. When it starts to rise up within us, we push it back down by closing our heart to it. The collision of sad energy coming up with closed energy pushing down creates all that anxious tension in the chest. Therefore, when we open our heart, the tension evaporates and our sadness rises higher in our body. As it gets above the chest, we often transmute it into anger at the last moment and expel it through aggressive words or actions. However, if we allow it to remain sadness, we'll feel its journey upward toward our eyes. A lump in our throat, perhaps. Then that prickly, swollen feeling in our nose and sinuses. Then pressure at the back of the eyes. Then, finally, tears.

The next week she told me a church service tenderized her to the point of tears. "Luckily, though," she said, "I got through it without totally breaking down, but I've almost burst into tears half a dozen times since Sunday."

She was acquainted with the sump pump metaphor, so I suggested her effort to avoid a "total breakdown" was akin to bailing water out of her basement one bucket at a time. Up the stairs, out the front door, dump it in the yard, repeat. The effort is exhausting, not to mention you can't keep up with the seepage that way. This is how we develop the idea that sadness is an unproductive emotion.

The advertising for a new book on emotional intelligence declares, "Sadness drains us of energy." No, it doesn't. The *suppression* of sadness drains us of energy, sometimes to the point of depression. "What is not ex-pressed is de-pressed," writes poet Mark Nepo.[2] So, sure, try the buckets first, but when they don't work, don't get defeated by it.

Instead, dislodge the debris from your float switch.

Phase 3: Sadness when it first flows again. When I began my own therapy in my early thirties, I hadn't cried in more than a decade, and the counseling made me aware of the debris firmly lodged on my float switch. Then, one night, my wife and I watched a film called *Lars and the Real Girl*, in which Ryan Gosling plays a young man devastated by loneliness after the death of his mother. Apparently delusional, he orders a blow-up doll from the internet and begins to act like she's his girlfriend. His small, supportive community loves him enough to play along. When my wife asked me what I thought of the movie, I opened my mouth to give my review, but my sadness came out instead.

Harvard brain scientist Dr. Jill Bolte Taylor teaches that "it takes less than 90 seconds for [any emotion] to be triggered, surge through our body, and then be completely flushed out of our blood stream."[3] She calls this the 90-Second Rule. "The healthiest way I know to move through an emotion effectively," she says, "is to surrender completely to that emotion when its loop of physiology comes over me. I simply resign to the loop and let it run its course for 90 seconds. Just like children, emotions heal when they are heard and validated."[4]

This holds true for the sorrow we've been carrying around for years as well. When we allow this pain to flow out unimpeded for the first time in years, the first few seconds of it often come with some powerful sensations. First, it feels so intense you fear it might eviscerate you. It won't. Second, it feels so bottomless you fear it might go on forever. It won't. Ninety seconds is all it will last.

The night my emotional sump pump started working again, the tears felt at first like they might tear me apart, the way violent vomiting feels like an assault on every muscle in your body. They didn't, though. Neither did they last more than ninety seconds. What they did do was leave me feeling as inwardly dry as I've ever felt. Hollowed out. The empty feeling was scary, and I wondered if it was the harbinger of depression. The next morning, however, I woke to a world that was suddenly displayed in high definition. The colors were brighter. The edges sharper. A week later, I started writing regularly for the first time in my life. A few months later I started a blog. And here we are.

One must be emptied in order to be filled.

Phase 4: Sadness when it's regular again. When I hobble into the massage session on my birthday morning, my massage therapist gets one look at me and gets the gist of it. "We'll start by passively stretching you," she says. She shows me to the table, lifts my right leg, and slowly bends it toward my upper body. Mid-stretch, she says gently, "Stop it."

"Stop what?" I ask.

"You're bending your leg for me. That's an active stretch. *I'm* going to passively stretch *you*. You don't do anything. You just let me take care of you."

And with those words, my pump kicks on. I can feel the sorrow rise upward through my chest and to the backs of my eyes. I have a decision to make: I can keep my finger on the float switch or let it rise.

"Are you okay if I cry?" I ask her.

"Of course," she replies as she lowers my right leg and lifts my left.

So I begin crying, quietly and gently. There is not a lifetime of sadness to expel like there was that first time in my thirties. It's just a trickle compared to that torrent. More and more, this is how it works once your sump pump is working properly again. The tears tell you there's sadness down there, and you just let them happen. Indeed, you welcome them, because you know they are freeing you. You are now in the "weeping mode," as Father Richard Rohr refers to it: "The 'weeping mode' is a different way of being in the world. It's different than the fixing, explaining, or controlling mode. We're finally free to feel the tragedy of things, the sadness of things. Tears cleanse our eyes both physically and spiritually so we can begin to see more clearly. . . . The way we can tell our tears have cleansed us is that afterwards we don't need to blame anybody, even ourselves. It's an utter transformation and cleansing of the soul."[5]

As I continue to cry, I become aware of a question being whispered within me over and over again. It's being asked in the sad, scared voice of the little boy I once was. As I cry, I hold space for him to feel his pain and to ask the question that's on his mind: "Who's going to take care of me?"

"We are commanded to love our neighbors as ourselves," writes Frederick Buechner, "and I believe that to love ourselves means to extend to those various selves that we have been along the way the same degree of compassion and concern that we would extend to anyone else. If to do so is unseemly, then so much the worse for seemliness."[6]

For about ninety seconds, I let that little boy in me feel once again the fullness of his loneliness. He cries quietly like he used to cry as a kid in his bed at night. In other words, I become like a child again while also remaining the adult I am, so he has a safe space in which to open his heart and release again a little more of the pain he's been carrying for both of us.

Elsewhere, Buechner writes, "Whenever you find tears in your eyes, especially unexpected tears, it is well to pay the closest attention. They are not only telling you something about the secret of who you are, but more often than not God is speaking to you through them of the mystery of where you have come from and is summoning you to where, if your soul is to be saved, you should go to next."[7]

You don't understand your way to feeling, you feel your way to understanding.

An Open Heart: Peace in Three Parts

I would change almost nothing about Elisabeth Kübler-Ross's stages of grief except for the name of the final stage: acceptance. Acceptance sounds like something you might do when you order a quarter pounder with cheese and they forget the cheese—you could wait in line again and get the correct sandwich, or you could accept it and eat your lunch. What happens after you feel your great pain, however, is so much more than acceptance. It's an inner calm, like a vast ocean that has misplaced its waves. And in place of those waves, three deeply peaceful experiences rise to the surface of you: energy, safety, and resilience.

Energy. "It happened," a friend tells me. "I was talking to my brother about our childhood, and in the middle of it I felt all this stuff welling up inside me. Instead of pushing it back down like I've been doing since we were kids, I opened my heart to it and let it flow. I thought it was going to be the end of me."

"And?" I ask.

"And I woke up the next morning with more energy than I've experienced in my entire life. Man, I felt weightless. When my son started crying at breakfast, I didn't get annoyed like

I usually do. I was just right there in his pain with him." He smiles like a sunrise. "Then, after I dropped the kids at school, I got an idea for a new business."

An already high-achieving client asks me, "What's the point of facing my past and feeling my pain?"

"Because until you do," I say, "you're only operating at a fraction of your full power."

A couple months later, his pump kicks on for the first time since he was eight years old, and he finds out exactly what I meant.

It takes a tremendous amount of emotional energy to keep your pain trapped inside of you. When you open your heart to that pain and let it flow out, the energy you've been using to keep your heart closed is freed up for other things. Furthermore, you've regained full access to your childlike soul and all its vitality and vibrancy, intuition and creativity, tenderness and compassion.

You might say it feels like entering the kingdom of heaven.

Dutch author Etty Hillesum writes, "You must be able to bear your sorrow; even if it seems to crush you, you will be able to stand up again, for human beings are so strong. . . . And if you have given sorrow the space it demands, then you may truly say: life is beautiful and so rich. So beautiful and so rich that it makes you want to believe in God."[8]

Safety. When my pump kicked on after *Lars and the Real Girl*, I was a young clinical psychologist fresh out of grad school. A trained scientist. A researcher by trade. I valued hard evidence. So "inner child" stuff had seemed woo-woo and froufrou to me. That night, though, my inner child became very real to me. **There is a difference between crying *for* your inner child and crying *as* your inner child.** I had cried *as* my inner child, and it made it impossible to deny his existence any longer.

The popular therapeutic framework called Internal Family Systems (IFS) was first pioneered in the 1980s by Dr. Richard

Schwartz, a family therapist who noticed many of his clients talked about distinct "parts" of themselves. According to Schwartz, our inner child is our original "exiled" part. "Before we get hurt," he writes, "they are the delightful, playful, creative, trusting, innocent, and open parts of us that we love to be close to. They are also the most sensitive parts, so when someone hurts, betrays, shames, or scares us, they are the parts who take in the extreme beliefs and emotions (burdens) from those events the most."[9]

Then, according to Schwartz, we develop two kinds of "protector" parts to rescue the inner child from those emotions. First, our "manager" parts are responsible for preventing that kind of pain from ever happening again. Next, when the managers fail, our "firefighter" parts swoop in to extinguish the emotion as fast as possible. In the end, though, this avoidance of sadness doesn't feel like more safety; it feels like more fear.

By allowing your sump pump to kick on again, you're not saving your inner child *from* their sadness, you're seeing your inner child *in* their sadness. This brings their time in exile to an end. They come home to wholeness. As your exiled inner child is welcomed back into your awareness, they begin to feel supported and safe, accepted just the way they are, perhaps for the first time ever.

When our heart closes, it's often because the child inside of us feels the mortal danger of separation and loneliness. That's why our adult reactions often don't match our adult circumstances—they're not a reaction to our adult circumstances. Therefore, the safety you create for your younger self is the safety you'll feel as your current self.

Resilience. When you fall off your bike and injure yourself, you don't get back on the bike because you're guaranteed to never fall again. In fact, it's quite the opposite: You get back on knowing you probably will fall again, yet also knowing you can survive a fall. This is what it means to live resiliently: You know life will hurt, but you choose to open yourself up to it anyway because you know you can handle the hurt. You've learned to feel your pain, so you no longer have to spend your life protecting yourself from it.

That's peace. That's freedom.

"There are many things that can only be seen through eyes that have cried," writes Catholic priest Óscar Romero.[10] The thing you feared would destroy you didn't destroy you; it strengthened you. You've turned pro at processing pain in real time, so you need not avoid that pain in yourself or in the world anymore. Your range of motion and emotion has expanded because you know you can go through the worst the world has to offer and still feel Okay. Not *okay* with a lowercase *o*. That kind of okay means you're happy or content or maybe numb to it all. This is a different kind of Okay. It's an Okay that is not a feeling within you but a truth about you. You can handle it. You've got what it takes.

You can keep your heart open in the most triggering situations.

You can choose calm at the crossroads of the past and the present.

You can truly show up to your life, ready for real connection.

Exercise: The Three Questions Visualization

Henry's mom was in a psychiatric hospital when he was a third grader.

In one of our first appointments, he'd told me his parents weren't perfect, but they did the best they could, and he knew they loved him. I was sure it was true. Part of the truth, at least. His mom was clinically depressed. That was more of the truth.

During the appointment in which Henry revealed it, he'd stayed in that bigger truth for a while. He talked about how distracted she was around his early successes, how disturbed she was by his adventures, and how he'd get home from school to find her asleep in her bedroom. Then, one day, after school, she was gone altogether.

"Your mom isn't happy," his dad explained, "so she's in a place where they make people happy again. In the meantime, we're gonna be happy the way two fellas like us deserve to be happy, aren't we?"

Henry had questions, but every time he asked one, his dad would change the subject with a joke, or a tickle match, or a milkshake. She was gone for months. When his dad traveled, he'd stay with his grandmother, whose mood was darker than ever.

For the next few appointments, Henry avoided any more discussion of his mother. Then one day he blew up at Owen again, and Sarah used the d-word: divorce.

"She says I'm getting nowhere and she's running out of patience," he says to start our call, looking more haggard than I've ever seen him. "And she's right. Every time she says something even remotely not-happy, I just shut down."

We'd discussed the sump pump a couple of weeks ago. He can guess what I'm thinking now.

"I know, I know, Doc," he says, raising his arms in mock surrender, "but I just can't get myself to take my finger off the float switch. Every time I feel anything rise up in me, I shut it down. It's a habit, and I can't seem to break it."

"Well, what if instead of waiting for it to come up, we went down into it?"

He issues some combination of a grunt, a groan, and a scoff. "That sounds perfectly miserable, but sure."

He is well-versed in the Margin for Terror exercise by now, so I ask him to close his eyes and to visualize the most recent scene in which he shut down with Sarah. I tell him to stay with it until he can feel that lead weight in his belly. He says he can. "Describe it to me again," I say.

"It's a big, black ball."

"Smooth, like an actual ball?" I ask.

"No. It's more like a black ball of gunk. Like tar. It moves slowly. Like rotating on an axis."

"Good," I say, before walking him through the breathing exercise. As Henry breathes space around the black ball of gunk, he's as close as he's ever been to this pain. He's about to go much closer.

"Now, I want you to picture a door on that black ball. Can you see it?"

He starts to shake his head and stops. "Huh. Yeah, I see it."

"What does it look like?"

"It's a big, heavy oak door with a brass knob on it."

"Is the knob plain or ornate?"

"Plain," he says.

"When you're ready, try the knob to see if it's unlocked." At this point, some people will discover their door won't open. They're not yet ready for this kind of proximity to their pain. "It turns," he says.

"Go ahead and open it and step inside." His eyebrows crease and one cheek twitches. After a moment, I ask if he's entered.

"Yes."

"What do you see?"

"Well, at first it seemed pitch dark in here, but now I can see the windows have blackout curtains on them. A little bit of moonlight is coming in around the edges."

"Good observations," I affirm. "Now, can you see any of the corners of the room?"

"Yeah, I can see one."

"Okay, go ahead and walk over there. As you approach it, notice your younger self is huddled in the corner."

On my screen, Henry flinches as if he's been gently slapped.

"Can you see him?" I ask.

If he can't, he may not be ready for this. Henry nods, though. He does see him. He is ready.

"Can you describe him to me?"

There is a long silence. Henry tries to speak and stops. He clears his throat and tries again.

"He's wearing a black Batman T-shirt and some gym shorts. It's what he always wears to bed."

"How old is he?"

"He's nine." Again, no hesitation. Deep down, we all know the age of the inner child that needs us the most.

"What else do you notice about his appearance?"

"Well, his hair's too long, for starters. He hasn't had it cut in a while. Since before."

"Before what?"

His voice grows quieter as he says, "Since before Mom went to the hospital."

"Do you notice anything else about him?"

"Yeah," he says. There's a nasally quality to his words now. The feelings are up to his sinuses. "He's just so sad, and by himself is the only place he can feel sad. And . . ."

"And?"

"And he's afraid."

"Afraid of what?"

Henry's voice hitches. "Afraid if he feels sad, he's going to be sent to a hospital too."

It's time for the first question. "I'd like you to ask him what he needs from you," I say. "Can you do that?"

On the screen, Henry's eyes are still closed, but he nods ever so slightly. There is a long silence. He swipes at something underneath his nose.

"When you're ready, you can tell me what he said."

Henry clenches his jaw, and when he speaks, all the steel is back in his voice. "He needs me not to tell anyone he's sad."

"Good," I say, segueing to the second question. "Now, ask him what he needs even *more* than that."

Another long pause, and this time when Henry speaks, all the metal has left his voice again, replaced by a quaver. "He wants me to tell him that he's going to be okay."

It never ceases to amaze me. Those three words. "You are Okay." Not "You're amazing." Not "You're worthy." Not "You're loved." Just the three words that our wounded inner child is always longing to hear: "You are Okay."

Henry is crying quietly now, though he's wiping furiously at his eyes, as if to rebuke himself for the tears. He's still got his finger on the float switch, and that's okay. Today probably won't be the day his pump kicks on all the way. But it's a step in that direction. As the tears slow and he begins to collect himself, I ask the third question.

"Now, ask him what he needs from you the *most*."

I was wrong. Today is the day. Henry's shoulders begin bouncing up and down with the sadness as it's ejected. Then his head disappears from the screen as he bends over and wraps his hands over it, like he's in a tornado drill. The camera shakes as his body, racked by sobs, jostles the desk in front of him. It's mostly silent, except for the sound of my voice.

"Just let it flow," I say quietly.

I whisper reassurances like that for about ninety seconds, until Henry raises his head. His face glistens with sorrow. He wipes it off onto his shirt sleeves.

"What does he want from you the most?" I ask.

"He asked me to hold him while he cries."

"Did you do that?"

Henry nods.

"Did he say anything else?"

"He asked me . . ." Henry pauses, trying to collect himself once more. "He asked me to never leave him again." His attempt to collect himself fails, as the pump kicks on again. Thirty seconds this time, and already gentler. I wait until he's wiped his eyes once more.

"And what did you say to him?"

Henry breathes for a while before responding. "I told him I'll be here whenever he needs me." Finally, Henry knows how to handle his sadness.

He's ready to show up to his life. He's ready for real connection.

PART III

GET CONNECTED

Do what you do with another human being, but never put them out of your heart.

Kabir

7

Set Boundaries Without Battles

> The love that consists in this: that two solitudes protect and border and salute each other.
>
> Rainer Maria Rilke

When I was growing up in the '80s, learning how to ride a bike wasn't just fun—it was freedom. Suddenly, you were no longer restricted to your yard or even your neighborhood. You could roam. One of the places I roamed to was a Wonder Bread bakery where, for chump change, you could buy a glazed pocket of dough filled with chocolate pudding. In the morning. Did you hear that? You were free to have dessert in the *morning*.

Similarly, there are ways in which you are suddenly free to show up as an adult once you've learned to keep your heart open in the midst of your triggers—once you're no longer forced to source your security from a closed heart. Setting healthy boundaries is one of the best forms of freedom.

It's the pudding pocket of openheartedness.

We're So Afraid

My wife's family is in town, and I've given all my extroverted energy to them. I'm badly in need of some introvert time, but it's hard to say no to people you love when they're only with you for a short time. Nevertheless, I'm running on empty, so I decide to kill two birds with one stone by waking up before dawn to combine my introvert and exercise time.

I'm about ten minutes into a quiet workout when my seven-year-old nephew materializes out of nowhere. He's eager to resume our pretend play from the night before, which had featured smoothies made from various kinds of animal poo. "Poothies," we'd called them. I'm in the middle of some squats when he shows me a rare specimen of "dinosaur poo," which looks exactly like a plastic banana.

I hold the boundary around my personal time and tell him I can't play.

He slinks off, grabs a ping-pong paddle, and begins the most pathetic solo play I've ever seen. He hits the ball across the table to no one, and it rolls under a bookcase. He walks to retrieve it, dragging his heels as if carrying a great burden, and repeats the process in the opposite direction. The ball comes to rest beneath the furnace. As he reaches into the tumbleweeds of dust beneath it, he glances at me with the glummest of faces, as if to say, "Look what you've reduced me to."

It works—I'm feeling terrible about my boundary.

Several minutes later, in the middle of some walking lunges, he appears in my path. "Hey, Uncle Kelly," he says, with forced nonchalance, "do ya wanna play some ping-pong with me?"

But I hold strong. "No, dude, not right now." It comes out more tersely than I intended, and I can see I've stung him with my tone. His shoulders slump as he turns away. It makes me want to relinquish my boundary even more, which agitates me all the more.

I lunge-walk to my phone and send my wife a text: *Can u please come get your nephew from the workout room?* It's a tantrumy little message.

Years ago—before I understood the nature of the heart—I would have chastised myself for acting childish. Now, I can see I'm simply closing my heart to my nephew because I'm afraid if I open my heart to him, I'll open my boundary to him as well. It's a common fear. Spiritual teacher Ram Dass describes it this way: "We're so afraid that if we open our hearts we won't be able to set limits, that if we open our hearts we're going to end up hurting ourself. I'll tell you, we're hurting ourselves . . . a lot more by not opening our hearts. We are starving to death in our protective security. And how secure do you feel?"[1]

Not very secure, I guess, if I feel threatened by a seven-year-old kid with some imaginary dinosaur dung.

The poet Kabir taught, "Do what you do with another human being, but never put them out of your heart."[2] Do what you do with another human being. Set your boundaries . . . or don't. Speak your truth . . . or don't. Forgive the frustrating flaws in people . . . or don't. But never put them out of your heart.

You can let them into your soul, even if you won't let them into your living room.

Hearts and Boundaries: The Interdependence Intersection

Every relationship is an ongoing negotiation of closeness versus distance. If you want to test that assertion, tell your wife—who generally wants more connection with you—that you're going to tag along on her girls' night out, and watch what she does. Or ask your son—who generally craves your attention—what he thinks of the cute new transfer student in his calculus class, and notice the color he turns. We are, all of us, all the time, seeking the sweet spot of intimacy, somewhere between the extremes of abandonment and engulfment.

Your heart and your boundaries are two very different ways of seeking that sweet spot. **The state of your heart is an inner condition, while the setting of your boundaries is an outer action. They aren't parallel roads. They're an intersection.**

Furthermore, that sweet spot actually has a name—it's called interdependence—though few of us know how to find it. I've created a framework that will show you how. It's called the Interdependence Intersection (see fig. 7.1). The horizontal axis represents the regulation of closeness versus distance with the outer action of boundary setting. Meanwhile, the vertical axis represents the regulation of closeness versus distance with the inner condition of our heart.

Figure 7.1

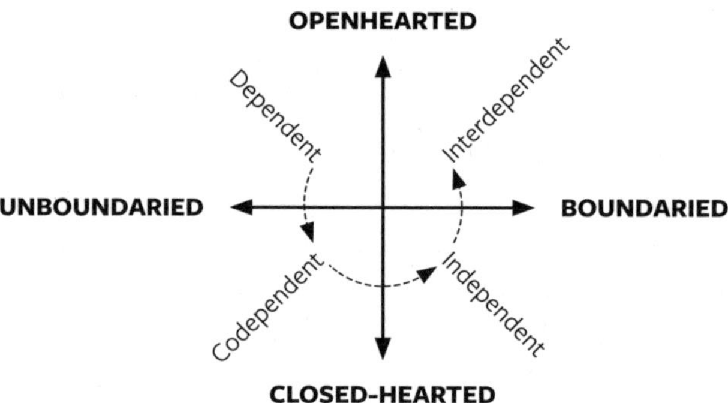

Like any intersection, this one has four corners—in this case, the four kinds of relationship styles created by the combination of outer action and inner condition: dependent (openhearted/unboundaried), codependent (closed-hearted/unboundaried), independent (closed-hearted/boundaried), and interdependent (openhearted/boundaried). This framework is like a new bike, helping you find the pudding pocket of openhearted relationships: interdependence.

Let's begin pedaling in the dependent corner of the intersection, because that is where every human life begins.

The Dependent Relationship Style

As an infant, the possibility of separateness is inconceivable, in part because all the bright lights and loud sounds and things that hurt are inconceivable at first, but also because separateness would mean death. Newly hatched snakes immediately slither off and start a life on their own. Newly hatched human beings, on the other hand, are absolutely dependent upon other human beings for survival. Closeness is essential. Distance would be fatal.

Of course, this state of union doesn't last forever. We all grow up. Though we do briefly plunge into it again when we fall in love.

The autumn I fell for my wife, I was an extreme introvert who suddenly lost any desire for alone time. I wanted to be with her all the time. My heart was wide open, and my boundaries evaporated completely. There was no me; it was all we, and we were one. For a moment in time, as you fall in love, you recapture that sense of total closeness from infancy. Yet, once again, it's just a passing mirage. The sense of separateness eventually returns and, along with it, the closeness versus distance dilemma.

Some of us manage that dilemma in codependent ways.

The Codependent Relationship Style

Many of the most likable people I know live in this closed-hearted/unboundaried corner of the intersection. They are, generally speaking, pretty miserable, but they are super-duper nice. They make the most supportive spouses, the easiest friends, the most compliant employees, and the most agreeable volunteers. Codependence often masquerades as saintliness.

Mental Health America, a national nonprofit organization dedicated to mental health, lists the following as some of the most common characteristics of codependency: fear of being abandoned or alone, doing anything to hold on to a relationship, a sense of guilt when asserting yourself, doing more than your share all the time, difficulty making your own decisions, and . . . problems setting boundaries.[3] The codependent assumption is that boundaries are bad because they create distance and thus increase the risk of abandonment. So, in a codependent relationship style, you strive for closeness by suppressing your differentness.

This suppression most commonly takes the form of poor boundaries. You have sex when you don't want to. You eat the pasta your friend serves, even though you have a gluten allergy. You take client calls at your nephew's bar mitzvah. Your actions are dictated far more by other people's wishes than your own. Emotional differentiation evaporates, as their feelings become your feelings. That old saying, "Not my circus, not my monkeys," doesn't apply to you—other people's "monkeys" are always making a mess in your mental living room.

Over time, however, this method for generating closeness becomes unsustainable. With each boundary you don't set, you become more resentful, so your heart becomes even more closed, and you become divided by your inner condition, if not your outer actions. By trying to find closeness without any room for distance, you fail to find either. When my nephew asked me to make poothies, my first impulse was a codependent one—I was tempted to suppress my boundary in favor of his wishes. However, before I even surrendered the boundary, I was already resenting him for it. This is the essence of codependence: resentment we cannot admit to about boundaries we cannot set.

The path from this kind of codependence to healthy interdependence almost always runs through independence.

The Independent Relationship Style

When you're first learning to drive a car, you don't practice on an open highway; you practice within the much safer confines of an empty parking lot. Similarly, when you first establish your sovereignty by setting a boundary, it's difficult to do so with an open heart. It feels overwhelming and dangerous. So, at first, most of us practice setting boundaries from within the much safer confines of a closed heart. In other words, our outer action changes before our inner condition can. When I sent my wife that tantrumy text about my nephew, I was setting a boundary with a closed heart.

This is how the codependent relationship style migrates into independence.

Some people don't migrate into independence, though, because it's always been their homeland. It's how they've related for as long as they can remember. They pride themselves on being unaffected by others. They source their sense of well-being from themselves only. They're self-sufficient, both emotionally and physically. And their boundaries are exceptionally clear: You do you, I'll do me. Independent boundaries may not be expressed angrily, but certainly bluntly—it's my way or the highway. This is a powerful position to be in, and that is precisely the point. Beneath the bravado of the independent relationship style, there's usually something else going on. In the same way a codependent style manages fear of abandonment, an independent style manages the fear of abandonment's *opposite*: engulfment.

An independent relationship style often begins with a childhood in which one's autonomy was unnecessarily stifled. The child was denied selfhood, physical space and safety, or emotional privacy. Therefore, they grew up feeling trapped, suffocated, or invaded. Now, the threat of engulfment creates as much or more anxiety than the threat of abandonment, so they double down on the distance in their relationships, both inwardly with a closed heart and outwardly with strong boundaries.

It rarely occurs to someone with an independent style that they can set their boundaries *while* opening their heart.

The Interdependent Relationship Style

Interdependence is a dance of closeness and distance.

A soul that feels at risk cannot dance. An inner child that feels unsafe cannot dance. A heart that is closed cannot dance. Only when you have done the work of opening your heart and feeling your way into the freedom of your foundational Okayness can you do the dance of interdependence in relationships. Only then do you feel totally safe moving apart from others and yet totally free moving back toward them. Only then are you resilient enough to trade the enmeshment of codependence or the detachment of independence for the engagement of interdependence.

"The opposite of control is not letting go," says Richard Rohr, "it's participation."[4]

Interdependence is participation. It's collaboration. For instance, while codependence takes total responsibility for the problems of another person, and independence dismisses others' problems as none of its business, interdependence is open to your problem becoming our problem, and vice versa.

"Yeah, but I didn't create their baggage," one client protested.

"No, but you can help them carry it," I responded.

I once pulled a muscle carrying an artificial Christmas tree out of the store. The box was clearly labeled "Team Lift." In interdependence, your problem is a team lift, and so is mine. We're separate from each other but supportive of each other. Always affected by the other but never devastated by them. Lending a hand without losing an arm and a leg.

"The conversation is the relationship," writes author and leadership expert Susan Scott.[5] In the interdependent relationship style, the opposite is also true: The relationship *is* a conversation. A dialogue. A pair of perspectives bantered and negotiated into something more whole. You don't try to dodge, win, or quit the conversation. You simply *have* the conversation.

How to Set Openhearted Boundaries: The "Yes, And" Conversation

When he was in the eighth grade, my son Aidan declared, "I think I know what I want to be when I grow up," with the confidence of someone who has just walked across hot coals at a Tony Robbins event.

My wife and I exchanged wary looks. He'd been sent to the principal's office yet again that week. The secretaries loved chatting with him, though. One of them suggested that if records were kept for number of office referrals, he'd be a candidate for the Guinness World Record. She laughed like we were all in on the joke. What kind of career might such a child choose?

"I'm going to be a comedian," he announced.

Yep. That's about right.

Four years later, he graduated from high school and moved to Chicago, working full-time to pay the bills while moonlighting for two years in the world-renowned Second City Comedy Club Conservatory. On the verge of graduating from Second City, his troupe was having a problem with a sketch in their graduation show.

"It just isn't working," he lamented. "It gets no laughs and kills the energy of the whole set." They'd workshopped it relentlessly behind the scenes but couldn't make it funny, and they didn't have a solid substitute for it. "I'm not sure if I even want you guys to come to the show," he admitted. They had one more practice performance before the big night.

A week later he called again. "We did it!" he exclaimed. "We figured it out. The whole show is solid now. I can't wait for you to see it next week."

"That's amazing, bud! How did you rewrite it?" I asked.

"We didn't rewrite it," he said. "We started the sketch like we always do, but I had an impulse to switch the order of the first two jokes, and I went with it."

"Wow, so *you* fixed it," I affirmed, like a good therapist-dad.

"No," he said, "*we* fixed it."

Then, he told me about the rule of agreement, also known as the Yes, And Rule. In their book *Yes, And: How Improvisation Reverses "No, But" Thinking and Improves Creativity and Collaboration*, Second City executives Kelly Leonard and Tom Yorton describe the rule:

> One actor offers an idea on stage, and the other actors affirm and build on to that idea with something of their own. Someone might say, for instance, "I've never seen so many stars in the sky." The actor sharing the scene has only one responsibility at this point: to agree with this, and add something new to it. So, that could be something like, "I know, things look so different up here on the moon." That simple statement affirms what the first actor offered, and added another idea. . . . In turn, this affirmation gives the first actor some information to build on and opens up a great many possibilities for the scene.[6]

Yes, And is the reason Aidan's improvisation at the beginning of the sketch worked. His fellow cast members didn't resist the unplanned change. They accepted it and went with it, and a new scene was written on the fly, one that was funnier than all their months of planning had been able to produce. Yes, And was foundational to fixing what wasn't working in their show.

It is also foundational to fixing what isn't working in our boundaries.

A boundary doesn't become a boundary until someone pushes back on it. And even then, it doesn't have to become a boundary right away. For someone with an interdependent relationship style, boundary setting is actually a relatively rare occurrence—not because boundaries are lax, but because they're often unnecessary. They are merely the third stage of a Yes, And conversation.

Stage 1: Wants

In the wants stage, a boundary is unrecognizable as a boundary because it is simply an expression of what you want. When you were a child, you wanted things. Then, you were taught your wants were bad, selfish, or inconvenient, so you quit expressing them. Here, you become childlike once again. You say what you want and listen to what others want.

When no one pushes back, your wants start dancing with each other.

Of course, most of us aren't on a professional improv stage when we express our wants. We're out here in the real world, where most people haven't yet heard about Yes, And. Our wants will be resisted. That's okay. Collaboration is a mindset—or a heartset, if you will. It is the spirit in which you choose to engage, even if those around you aren't in the same spirit. Just because someone else onstage is No, Butting doesn't mean you have to. You can lead the dance of interdependence with Yes, And, even if everyone else has two left feet.

So, when people push back, how do you decide if your want is actually a need? Put simply, **a need is any want that won't go away**. When a want grows into a need because it's been unacknowledged, unexpressed, or unsatisfied—or if you can foresee it being so—it's time to advocate for it.

Stage 2: Needs

In the needs stage, the degrees of difficulty increase, but the method remains the same: Yes, And. You are now restating what you want but clarifying how important it is to you. This is new information to the person hearing it, and it may make all the difference to them. Also, it might not. We may show up fully to our relationships—openheartedly expressing our carefully discerned needs—and people may ignore, dismiss, belittle, criticize, or overrule them. It's hurtful, but it's also normal.

When it happens, we now have the ability to notice our heart closing and to open it back up. This doesn't mean we abandon our need. It may still progress into a boundary, but it will be our choice, not our impulse.

When do you turn your need into a boundary?

You set a boundary when you can't keep your heart open without it. Now we've come a long way from being "afraid that if we open our hearts we won't be able to set limits," as Ram Dass observed earlier.[7] It's quite the opposite, actually: We set limits not because our heart has already closed but *so* we can keep our heart open.

Back in my days as an outpatient mental health therapist, I'd charge clients the full fee for missing an appointment without adequate notice. When I'd remind them of this boundary at the beginning of the next session, they'd often say, "You must be really angry with me if you're charging me." I'd respond, "No, I'm charging you so that I won't get angry with you."

Healthy boundaries aren't the result of a closed heart, they're the foundation of an open heart.

Stage 3: Boundaries

When you arrive at your boundaries through an open heart, they look different from the macho boundaries espoused in most social media memes. "If you're offended by my boundaries, then you're probably one of the reasons I need them," declares one frequently shared graphic. This is closed-hearted boundary setting. It assumes a battle before the boundary is even set.

In contrast, openhearted boundaries evolve the way electric fences have evolved in recent years.

When we got our first dog, there was only one option for an electric fence: It was a piece of hardware buried permanently beneath the ground. It was expensive and immovable. Now you can get a GPS collar for your dog and use an app to retrace the boundaries of the fence whenever and wherever you want. Openhearted boundaries work the same way. They are firm but also flexible. They are intentional but still negotiable.

Boundaries are not a duel but a dance.

In a good dance, you are sometimes very close and sometimes far apart. Healthy boundaries are guided by our wants and needs, which are constantly in flux, so our boundaries flow along with them. You don't dance the same way on different nights with different partners in different settings. When you dance, you do what your soul and the situation call for, while never putting the other person out of your heart.

Is there ever a time to set a fixed boundary, like the old-fashioned electric fences? Sure. In their book *Fight Right*, marriage experts Julie and John Gottman report finding three relationship situations in which boundaries shouldn't be redrawn. They are abuse, refusal to seek help for addiction, and differences about whether or not to have children.[8] Perhaps you'd add a few more to your list. Do so consciously.

And then dance with the rest.

Never Put Them Out of Your Heart

I'm in the middle of some crunches—and my nephew is staging what sounds like an epic battle with some *Star Wars* action figures—when I open my heart back up to him. I've been practicing openheartedness for several years now, and opening is becoming almost as natural as closing, so it happens quickly.

I let him in without letting go of my boundaries.

In doing so, I regain access to my own pain, and I become aware that I will now be a part of *his* wound. *The* wound, actually. The great pain we all encounter in childhood: the pain of separateness, of longing for the unity we are gradually losing. As I open to him, I don't feel guilty about this. I can't save him from the human condition. He will learn the pain of separateness one way or another. I did. You did. We all do. On this morning, it just so happens I'm his teacher.

With an open heart, though, I can be a loving teacher. So, I walk over to where he's rearranging poothie ingredients, squat down, and ask him to look me in the eye. He does. "Hey, bud," I say, "I bet it hurts that I won't play with you right now. But I want you to know I love you, I think you're awesome, and I can't wait to play again later."

His eyes swim as he throws his arms around me in a big hug, and he doesn't ask me to play again. Probably because he feels what it's like to be on the receiving end of an openhearted, interdependent boundary.

He's separate but not severed.

Admittedly, when it comes to degrees of difficulty, this openhearted boundary is about a two out of ten. I'm forty years older than him, and the stakes are low. It's just a morning exercise routine—not a particularly heavy lift, pun intended. There are certainly much more challenging tests of our ability to stay open internally while boundaried externally. Your parents will say they did the best they could and then keep on doing the same old hurtful things. Your kids will marry people who turn them against you. Your spouse will refuse to change. Your friends will pontificate about the virtues of the political party you deplore. Your neighbor's Christmas lights projector will cast dancing red and green dots all over your bedroom curtains until two in the morning. Also, they have a Pomeranian they allow to bark at all hours.

The intersections of our inward condition and our outer actions are countless. But, my oh my, that moment in which you open your heart and realize the relational realities weren't your prison, the closing of your heart to them was. That can turn any intersection into a transformation, as you discover the health of your boundaries depends not on the strength of your spine but the openness of your heart.

A few minutes later, my nephew is making poothies with both Luke Skywalker and Darth Vader—togetherness abounds—when my wife texts back, "Do you still need me to come get him?"

I pause my workout to write her back: "No, you don't need to. I grew up a little." I learned how to ride my bike to a better place: interdependence.

The pudding pocket of openheartedness.

Exercise: Yes, And Journaling

Sarah appears on my screen.

It's been nine months since her first appointment with Henry, and the living room behind her is still strewn with toys. The churn of childhood. This is her fifth individual appointment in as many weeks. After Henry's sump pump kicked on, he stopped criticizing her "dark side" and even started holding space for it. It made her want to explore the pain that might be holding her back from showing up more openheartedly as well.

It turns out that pain has a lot to do with growing up in a home where the adults were overwhelmed by life. Not abusive or even dysfunctional, really. Just dysregulated in a way that permeated the atmosphere of her young world. In the midst of it, she found calm by becoming the favorite child. The quiet caretaker. She closed her heart and kept her cares and concerns to herself. In other words, she became a professional codependent and was rewarded for it with her parents' affection.

They'd say, "Thank God for our Sarah. She's our easy one," oblivious to how that moniker can become a millstone around a child's neck.

It's no wonder Henry first experienced her as a perfect companion: At first, she didn't challenge any of his ambition and wanderlust. In the meantime, though, her marital resentment added to her childhood resentment, and the cracks in her codependency finally started to show.

Consequently, she erratically fluctuated between no boundaries and angry boundaries.

In the last five sessions, her sump pump hasn't run as intensely as Henry's did—she still has her finger on the float switch to some extent, probably fearing the implications for her relationship with her mother, who is still living and who she remains close with. However, her feelings have flowed enough to know Henry isn't solely responsible for her pain. And then she emailed me a few days ago with a single sentence:

"This week I want to focus on setting boundaries with my mom."

I introduce her to an exercise I call Yes, And Journaling. In this exercise, you role-play your conversation with another person, journaling your speaker turn with your nondominant hand and journaling the other's response with your dominant hand. Writing with the nondominant hand helps you get in touch with your most childlike wants and express them with the open heart they deserve.

Sarah is poised with pen in hand. Her left hand. I encourage her to start.

"I want," she says aloud for my benefit, and slowly because the writing is slow, "you . . . to . . . listen . . . to . . . me."

She looks up with a question in her eyes: *Did I do it right?* Technically, she didn't.

"It's a good start, but notice how your want is really a command, telling her what to do."

"Yikes, that's the dominating defense, isn't it?" She's a remarkable student.

"It is. And that's okay. It's just a sign that even here on Zoom, with your mother nowhere in sight, your heart is still at least a little closed to this kind of conversation with her." I guide her through the Margin for Terror exercise again, and she reports her heart is more open. I instruct her to express the most soulful version of her first request. She tears up a bit, so I know she's getting to it. She puts her head down to write.

"I just want . . . to feel . . . heard."

When she looks up this time, there's no question in her eyes, just tears. One escapes from her lower lid, and she wipes it away with her dominant hand.

"Beautiful," I say. "Now you can switch hands and write your mother's response." This usually comes relatively quickly. Indeed, for Sarah, it does.

"Oh honey, you and I talk all the time. I'm always hearing you," Sarah says aloud as she writes it.

"That sounds very real," I say. "She means well, but she just doesn't get it, and why should she? You're expressing wants you've buried your whole life. Nevertheless, she negated your want, so now you get to decide whether it's a need and if so, you get to express it as such. Knowing what you know now, can you go back to being unheard in your key relationships, if that's what your mother wants?"

This doesn't require much discernment for Sarah. "No," she says, "I'm never going back."

Now it's her turn again. Her challenge is to Yes, And what her mother has said, while expressing her need. The pen switches hands again, but the writing doesn't start right away. Her dominant hand reaches for something off-screen and reappears with a tissue. She wipes her eyes and her nose. Our most soulful needs tend to come with the most sorrow attached to them. Sarah starts to write.

"Yes you hear . . . what I say . . . and I just need . . . to feel seen . . . for a while." She finishes writing it and blows her nose.

"It rings true," I say. "A teenager wants to be heard. A child just wants to be seen. When you're ready, you can write your mother's response."

The pen switches hands, and again her mother's response flows fast. "Oh my goodness, Sarah, what are you talking about? I have eyes. Of course I can see you."

"Can you let go of your need to be seen and still keep your heart open to her, Sarah?"

"I don't think so," she says. "Well, maybe. For a while. But I've been doing that my whole life. I don't want to do it anymore."

Sarah sets her Yes, And boundary before I can even suggest she do so.

"Yes you see me . . . like a friend . . . and I want you . . . to see me . . . like a daughter . . . because you are . . . the only person . . . on the planet . . . who can see me . . . that way."

She looks up at the screen, no questions in her eyes this time. You know an openhearted boundary when you've set one.

"If she's open to that, the rest of your relationship will be a collaboration between what you want and what she's learning to give."

Sarah, too, is on her way to the Wonder Bread store, where they're selling pudding pockets for chump change.

8

Stay Curious During Conflict

Once we believe in ourselves, we can risk curiosity, wonder, spontaneous delight, or any experience that reveals the human spirit.

Edwin McMahon and Peter Campbell

When you start showing up to your life with an open heart, you go through longer and longer seasons of internal peace and relational prosperity. You set boundaries without battles, and what used to become a divisive conflict becomes deeper connection. You've tapped into a calmer level of existence, where things are essentially Okay. You trust it. You go with it. You chuckle at the way you lived before: reacting to everything, resisting everything, rupturing everything. You'd be foolish to revert to those old ways.

Then, one day, you do.

It Sneaks Up on You

A perfectly good day can be ruined by getting into the Hall of Fame.

It's a Tuesday morning, and all is well with the world—which of course isn't true, but every once in a while it almost feels like it. The kids are at school, and their grades are good. My wife is happy (and, you know, happy wife, happy life). There's enough money in the bank account for things to go mildly wrong without causing too much stress. Say, a water heater—or, heaven forbid, a furnace—that needs to be replaced. Thanks to some healthy boundaries around my time, I've just enjoyed a productive writing session. My heart has every reason to be open, and it is. On mornings like this, I wonder if it will ever close again.

The email announcing that my high school golf team is being inducted into our school's athletic Hall of Fame comes as a welcome surprise, at first.

As a kid, golf was my greatest passion, and I was one of a dozen guys on the varsity team. In high school golf, six players compete in each match, and the top four scores are aggregated into the team total. My senior year, I played in every match, was in the top four scores almost every meet, and was named co-MVP. We finished seventh in the state. By contrast, my junior year, I was the seventh player on the team and never played in a varsity match. The team finished fourth at the state meet, where I tagged along as an alternate. No one got sick or injured, so I just spectated.

It's the junior year team that's being inducted into the Hall of Fame, including the six guys who played, and me.

The emails are flying back and forth as old friends with a reason to reconnect start trading jokes about the glory days. I respond with a quip of my own but immediately regret what I sent. I try to recover by responding to someone's recollection of our coach, but they're now reminiscing about the ridiculous things we did at the back of the bus while traveling to tournaments. I never find the rhythm and quit trying, but for the rest of the day I wish for a do-over. After my last appointment, I make the short commute from my home office to the kitchen, where my wife is getting dinner started. I'd texted her with the news earlier in the day.

"Congratulations!" she declares. "So, your senior team is being inducted into the Hall of Fame?"

I mumble, "Nah, junior team."

"Your junior team? I didn't think you played on that team."

"Well, that's the one being inducted," I snap back.

"Ooookay," she says, returning her attention to whatever she's stirring on the stove.

I'm aware I'm acting like a jerk. So, like a really good jerk, I double down. "What?" I ask as defensively as humanly possible.

"Nothing," she says, keeping her eyes on the pot, making it clear she's not going to interact with whatever this is.

What this is, clearly, is a closed heart.

However, it makes no sense. Let's just say my response to the group actually was a mistake. Who cares? Most days I commit blunders twice that size before breakfast and don't give it a second thought. My heart has been consistently open for months, through far more difficult situations than this one. Now, without warning, it is closed, and I'm acting more neurotic than I've acted in a long, long time.

The question is, *why?*

The Why-Question

"Why?" is a one-word question that can be asked in very different ways.

At the beginning of the Peaceful Pivot Process, when our heart was closed, the why-question was often asked with exasperation and frustration. There was some self-condemnation tucked into the tone. Our closing felt like a failure, and our interrogation of it sounded more like accusation than contemplation. Now, though, we're reconnected with our childlike soul, so we're free to ask "Why?" like a kid again. Kids ask "why" not because they're frustrated but because it's fun. In his memoir, *The Anthropocene Reviewed*, bestselling novelist John Green describes the "Why?" game his kids like to play:

> I'll tell them, for instance, that I need them to finish the breakfast, and they'll say, "Why?"
>
> And I'll say so that you receive adequate nutrition and hydration, and they'll say, "Why?" And I'll say because as your parent I feel obligated to protect your health, and they'll say, "Why?" And I'll say partly because I love you and partly because of evolutionary imperatives baked into my biology, and they'll say, "Why?" And I'll say because the species wants to go on. . . .
>
> And then there will be a silence. A blessed and beautiful silence will spread across the breakfast table. I might even see a kid pick up a fork. And then, just as the silence seems ready to take off its coat and stay awhile, one of my kids will say, "Why?"[1]

When your heart closes, don't get cranky about it, get curious about it, like a kid. A closing heart isn't a deficiency; it's an opportunity to learn more about yourself, to become more whole and maybe even a little more healed. As you show up to your life more openheartedly, you'll begin to see any failure to stay open as an X on a map. You know there's treasure buried beneath the X, and you want to dig for it.

"Why?" is the shovel with which you dig.

There may be no better illustration of this principle than Biosphere 2, a three-acre terrarium launched on September 26, 1991, in the Arizona desert.[2] As a prototype for a self-sustaining colony on another planet, it was designed to be a hermetically sealed ecosystem where thousands of plants and animals would provide the human inhabitants with all the food, water, and air they needed.

Within a year, though, things were going very wrong.

For instance, oxygen levels were dangerously low, and carbon dioxide levels were dangerously high. However, because the Biosphere's investors wanted the project to be an unmitigated success, they refused to ask the why-question. Instead, they secretly covered up the problems by pumping oxygen into the habitat and using machines to scrub the environment of excess carbon dioxide. When these cheats were discovered, the project lost credibility and was panned in the press.

Then, in 1996, some curious scientists from Columbia University took over the Biosphere and started asking the why-question.

Quickly, they discovered the soil in the Biosphere was too rich in organic matter, so its thriving bacteria were using up too much oxygen and releasing too much carbon dioxide. Another example: The trees in the Biosphere were falling over. Why? It turns out, the roots of trees are strengthened every time the wind blows, so without wind stressing the trees, their root systems were too weak to keep the trees upright once they reached a certain size.

Before long, the scientists realized the value of the project was not in its perfection but in its failures—namely, what they could learn from those failures if they asked why. Now, twenty years later, Biosphere 2 plays a key role in humankind's race to understand climate change and its effect on Earth's ecosystems. In pivoting from a focus on its unequivocal success to curiosity about its flaws, those scientists were demonstrating something essential about the journey toward openhearted connection:

Everything that feels like a failure *of* progress is actually a focus *for* progress.

Soften to Your "Setbacks"

The morning after the Hall of Fame announcement, it's clear my heart is still closed.

My mind is still racing, wishing I could turn back time and revise those emails. I'm making guesses about how the guys are judging me. I keep speculating about how to repair my standing with them. Just a few years ago, before I was practicing openheartedness, I'd have gotten up and tried to distract myself with writing or tried to purge the bad feelings with a vigorous workout. Now, though, I'm not avoidant of a closed heart; I'm invigorated by it. Life has presented me with an unexpected opportunity to grow a little more. So, I find a quiet space where I can get curious.

And I let the "Why?" game begin.

Q: Why is my heart closed like this?

A: *It's trying to protect me.*

Q: Why? From what?

A: *I fear being rejected by the guys. Not belonging to the group.*

Q: Why?

A: *Because that was how I always felt that junior season. Like a tagalong. Like a younger sibling bothering his older brothers. Like I wasn't in on the joke. Like I was just on the outside of the inside. Like I didn't belong.*

Q: Okay, but that was thirty years ago. Why would you still feel that way now, when you belong to so many other people?

A: *Because my nervous system can't differentiate between a situation happening thirty years ago and a situation happening right now. Reconnecting with people from my past has triggered experiences from my past. And maybe that's a gift.*

Q: Why would that be a gift?

A: *Because my memories of those days are so vague. It's hard to remember what it was like to be sixteen-year-old me, and now I don't have to. I can actually feel it. In this moment, I'm actually inhabiting his mind and body.*

The "Why?" game ends there, as the sump pump kicks on again.

Sixteen-year-old me was scared—desperate to belong but, it seemed, always coming up short. He'd fall asleep at night wondering what he might have done wrong today to jeopardize his belonging tomorrow. You'd never have known it by looking at him in the morning, though. He could flash the smile you wanted to see from him. He could make you feel the way you wanted to feel. And he could tag along with the guys for a whole golf season and stay at just the distance he guessed you wanted him to be. He could spectate.

As the pump kicks on, it's tempting to put my finger on the float switch yet again in the most caring of ways: by giving sixteen-year-old me a pep talk. "Hey dude, no need to feel so bad. In thirty years, you're going to have a wonderful wife, three amazing kids, a bunch of good friends, and—believe it or not—tens of thousands of online followers." This type of reframe is at the center of most mindset coaching, much of the self-help movement, and a lot of spiritual bypassing disguised as gratitude. The motto is: Focus on what helps, not what hurts. The goal is to overcome your "limiting beliefs." However, no matter how much we overcome them in the moment, our limiting beliefs always come roaring back, usually even more intensely than before, and there's a reason for that.

It's not a limiting belief, it's your inner child.

The power of positive thinking is meaningless to the younger versions of you for a couple of reasons. First, in the same way telling a kid who has skinned their knee that it won't hurt a day from now does nothing to ease the sting in the moment, telling your sixteen-year-old self that being forty-seven isn't so bad does nothing to change the sting of being sixteen. Second, that younger version of you will always be young. Sixteen-year-old me will always be sixteen. He's frozen in the timelessness of my nervous system.

In that sense, we human beings are just like a tree, growing a new ring for every year of our life, and those rings are with us forever.

Dendrochronologists can tell a great deal about what a tree has been through by looking at a cross section of the tree and the rings it reveals. Wider rings mean cooler and wetter seasons of life. Narrow rings mean hotter and dryer. You can see traumas, such as forest fires, in the rings of a tree. But a tree doesn't become a tree by healing its rings or changing its rings or removing its rings. A tree becomes itself by being the sum total of its rings. A tree inhabits its full tree-ness when it simply stands there and sways, its roots and all its rings making it possible to withstand the wind.

The sixteenth ring of me will always be afraid of not belonging. He's lonely and will always be lonely. He's sad and will always be sad. So, I don't try to motivate him out of his sadness. I just stay with him in the midst of it.

A friend of mine recently won a Most Valuable Participant award at an annual men's conference and was invited to give an acceptance speech.

"I showed up here authentically and vulnerably," he said, "and I love myself for that. However," he continued, "a part of me also feels ashamed because I don't think I deserve this award."

He took a long pause. You could hear a pin drop.

"I love that part of me too," he said.

He wasn't done.

"There's also a part of me that feels anxious, because I think I've got to live up to this honor from now on. I love that part of me too. And there's a part of me that feels like I'm better than you all because I won this award. I love that part of me too." He went on and on, loving every ring.

When you can love every version of you—for who you needed to be in order to weather that season of life—there is no part of you left out of your love. The sixteenth ring of me was scared and ashamed and lonely. And I love that part of me too. Showing up openheartedly to your life means loving every ring you've ever been, because they're all here now.

Every closing is merely another opportunity to ensure that you leave no ring of you unloved.

Stop Debating, Start Debriefing

In his memoir, *The Healing Path*, psychotherapist and spiritual teacher James Finley writes:

> It is in experiencing and accepting how difficult it can be to free ourselves from our hurtful attitudes and ways of treating ourselves and others that we begin to understand that the healing path is not a linear process in which we can force our way beyond our wounded and wounding ways. Rather, it is a path along which we learn to circle back again and again to cultivate within ourselves a more merciful understanding of ourselves as we learn to see, love, and respect the still-confused and wounded

> aspects of ourselves. Insofar as these [parts] recognize that they are seen, loved, and respected in such a merciful way, they can feel safe enough to release the pain they carry into the more healed and whole aspects of ourselves.[3]

No matter how long you go between triggers, another trigger will always present itself. You will close. On the road less triggered, you show up to the closing with curiosity instead of condemnation and create another opportunity to get to know your inner child. Then, this kind of curiosity goes viral, and you start extending it to your people.

Perhaps you were looking forward to dinner with a good friend, but when you arrived at the restaurant, something was a little off in their greeting. They weren't as exuberant as usual. They were unusually deferential about the appetizer order. They were distracted throughout the conversation. In the past, you might have personalized their behavior and gotten defensive, or blamed them for whatever their problem might be.

Now, having practiced curiosity within yourself, your first instinct is to be curious about them.

Which of their rings has been triggered? Is this what it was like to be with them when they were eight, or eighteen, or twenty-eight? Maybe you inquire about it, maybe you don't. However, instead of feeling spiteful that you were subject to an off night with them, you feel grateful that you got to time travel with them.

Then you get home, and your spouse is clearly triggered by something. They're keeping you at arm's length, both physically and emotionally. You rack your brain for what you might have done wrong. Nothing comes to mind. In the past you might have begun preparing for a debate about why you're being treated unfairly. Now, you just get curious.

You don't debate what is happening, you debrief what is hurting.

You ask the why-question with sincere curiosity, and perhaps you discover—after twenty years of episodes exactly like this one—when your partner pushes you away, they are actually feeling abandoned by you. They're managing their sense of rejection by reciprocating it. You ask what ring this is. They tell you it's probably their fifteenth ring. You tell them you love their fifteenth ring too.

And now you're just two trees bending in the wind, growing stronger with every gust.

Become the Whole Tree

A few months after the Hall of Fame announcement, the day has arrived. Six of the seven of us will be at a private induction ceremony in the afternoon, followed by a public introduction between that evening's basketball games.

Throughout the morning, I catch myself calculating how I want to show up in order to ingratiate myself to the guys. In other words, my forty-seven-year-old self watches my sixteen-year-old self plotting his path to belonging. I don't try to silence him or fix him or convince him to see things differently. I just let him be what he is—the sixteenth ring of me—and I promise him I'll love him throughout the day. It is in this opening of my heart to him that I become *more* than him.

I become the whole tree, one with forty-seven rings and roots strengthened by the winds of time.

The joyous reunion at the induction ceremony reminds me that my belonging was far less tenuous than my sixteen-year-old self feared. This was my band of brothers, and, in our school's 130-year history, our four years were golf's golden era: three conference championships, three regional championships, a sectional championship, and two back-to-back top-ten state finishes. We *did* that, and we had fun together while we were doing it, my sixteen-year-old insecurity notwithstanding.

We hadn't been warned to prepare a speech for the induction ceremony, so fortunately I'm the last in line and have a little time to reflect as my teammates offer their words. When I'm handed the mic, I remind those gathered that parents and kids have very different concerns on the first day of high school. As parents, we hope they'll get good grades, feel mostly happy, and, above all, avoid teen pregnancy. However, a fourteen-year-old entering high school has only one question repeating like a drumbeat in their mind:

Who will I belong to?

Who will I belong to?

Who will I belong to?

"The hallways aren't a great place to sort that out," I say, "but when you get on the practice field or the basketball court or, in our case, the golf course, you breathe a sigh of relief. You've found your people. So, I want to thank everyone who makes athletics possible in our school district. You're not just giving kids a game to play, you're giving them a place to belong." My sixteen-year-old self marvels that I can reel off a speech like that.

A few hours later, we walk onto the basketball court to applause from the home crowd. I see at the top of the bleachers some beloved neighbors from childhood. My sixteen-year-old self is grateful for them. I see the gentleman I worked for every summer in college. He was the best of bosses. My twenty-two-year-old self is grateful for him. And I see my daughter in the band section. Her clarinet is resting in her lap so she can use both hands to make a heart symbol at me. I hold up my hands and return the heart symbol. My forty-seven-year-old self is grateful for her.

When the announcements are done and the applause dies down, I don't want to walk off the court.

It's not the honor of it I want to bask in. It's the coming-full-circle-ness of it. It's that feeling of being the whole tree, with all its rings fully present at once. It's that sensation that time machines do exist, and you are one of them, having retrieved every version of yourself, gathering all of them in this one place and this one moment.

It's the peaceful awareness, articulated by the poet Walt Whitman, that we, each of us, contain multitudes.

Exercise: The Five Whys Interview

Henry and Sarah appear on my screen in the same frame.

I've been alternating individual appointments with each of them, and it's the first time I've seen them together since Sarah found out Henry was bailing on their hiking plans to play golf with a business prospect. That was many months ago. Now they are sitting at their kitchen counter, and the living room behind them is tidier than usual. Henry just said something to make Sarah laugh. He's clearly pleased with himself. She's clearly open to him. Their shoulders rest against each other.

Eventually, Henry notices me. "Oh, hey, Doc, sorry to keep you waiting," he says.

I tell them they never have to apologize for being openhearted in front of me. Nor closed-hearted, for that matter. They laugh.

"Doc, thanks to you, it's been weeks since our hearts closed to each other. It's starting to feel like when we first met. I mean, it's not the exact same, of course. Kids and businesses and all that. But it's not different, either, if you know what I mean." I do.

"And you'd be proud of me, Dr. Kelly," Sarah adds. "I've been setting better boundaries with my mom. I'm saying what I want while keeping my heart open, and it's making a difference." A thought passes over her eyes, and she laughs. "I've still got a ways to go, though. I just remembered Owen has a game on Saturday, and I really want to be there, but she asked me to go antiquing with her, and I reflexively said yes. I hate antiquing." She rolls her eyes.

Meanwhile, it looks like someone has popped Henry's balloon.

"Honey," he says, aiming for gentle and missing the mark, "we're supposed to fly out Saturday morning for my conference in Phoenix. Remember, we agreed to go as a couple this time? It's been on the calendar for months."

Henry's tone has become more agitated as he speaks. Sarah has crossed her arms. I can already see red working its way up past the collar of her shirt, toward her chin. Their shoulders are no longer touching.

I notice right away the role reversal: Sarah has forgotten to prioritize their relationship this time, and it's Henry who feels hurt by it. This kind of role reversal is always a sign of progress. Open hearts are evolving hearts. Relationship dynamics shift. Sometimes they're even turned on their heads. It's no wonder the triggers sneak up on us right when everything seems to be going so well—there are a lot of moving parts.

"Oh good," I exclaim, with intentionally exaggerated enthusiasm. "Your hearts are closing! What a great opportunity to get curious about why!"

If they are solidly in part three of the Peaceful Pivot Process, they will be able to join me to some extent in my enthusiasm.

Henry softens quickly and smiles. "I can't believe I'm saying this, but yeah, I'm not afraid of this closing. We know what to do now. We always wind up stronger and healthier because of it. Why would this time be any different?"

His confidence clearly inspires a sense of safety in Sarah. Their shoulders are touching again.

"Ugh," she says. "This isn't how I wanted to spend this hour, but I can open my heart to what I don't want."

They are fully showing up for real connection.

"I think you guys are ready for the five whys interview," I say.

I can see the questions in their eyes.

"The five whys was a problem-solving technique created by Toyota in the 1930s and popularized in the '70s. The idea is you identify an issue and ask why it happened. Then you ask why *that* happened, and so on, until you've gotten to the root of the issue. After five whys, you're usually pretty close to it, though five isn't a hard-and-fast rule. You ask it as many times as you need to in order to satisfy your curiosity."

"You called it an interview?" Henry asks.

"Ah yes, good catch. The idea is that you can't treat the five whys like a back-and-forth conversation because you'll lose the thread. Instead, you decide which of you is going to be the curious interviewer and which of you will be the interviewee, and you stay in those roles until both parties have a sufficient understanding of what's happening. Does that make sense?" They nod. "So, who'd like to be the curious question-asker?"

Sarah jumps in. "I'd like to ask the questions. Henry usually loves traveling to these conferences alone. That's probably why I didn't take it seriously. I'd like to understand more about why it's different this time."

"Henry, does that sound okay with you?" I ask. He flashes a thumbs-up. "Go ahead and face each other," I say. They do. "Now, Sarah, you can begin by asking Henry why his heart just closed." Sarah repeats the question.

If Henry is triggered by her why-question, it may be a sign that there's still more work for him to do in part two of the process. He's not triggered, though. Rather, he replies instantly, "Because I wanted you to go with me."

"Why?"

"Because I like spending time with you."

Sarah starts to open her mouth and clamps it shut. She looks sideways at me. "Yikes, this is harder than it sounds. I'm not supposed to reply?"

"Is your reply a reflection of your curiosity or your own closing?"

She grimaces like she's been caught red-handed. "Closing," she confirms.

"Then go ahead and stick with the question. Draw on Yes, And here. Trust what he says is true *and* get curious about it rather than negating it."

She turns back to him. "Why do you want to spend time with me? All of a sudden," she adds, sneaking in a bit of what her closed heart wanted to communicate, in spite of her efforts.

"I've *always* loved being with you," says Henry.

Sarah is very slow to respond. Because she's turned sideways, I can't tell she's tearing up until she raises a hand to wipe something from her eye. What she says next is spoken with the kind of tenderness that can only come with true curiosity.

"Why have you acted otherwise for so long?"

Henry takes a long pause, closes his eyes, puts his hand on his chest, and breathes deeply. I've seen him do this in our individual sessions. He's calming himself for a brief inward journey, recovering his answer from somewhere deep within before he speaks.

"I've always wanted to be with you, but I've never been able to be with your dissatisfaction. It felt like my mom's depression to me, and depression meant separation. It wasn't you I was resisting in those moments, it was separation from you."

"Why now, then? What has changed?"

His answer comes quickly this time. "I can handle my feelings now, so I can also handle yours too. I'm learning that your discontent isn't a wall between us like it was between my mom and me. It's a bridge."

"Why haven't you told me this sooner?"

Henry tries to speak and then chokes on some surprise emotion. The sump pump has kicked on without warning. A gentle gush. He lets it, and she lets him. What he says next comes in on the tide of that emotion, his voice shaking.

"Because in a way, I'll always be a nine-year-old, lying awake in bed at night, thinking my mom is gone because she doesn't really want to be with me."

Sarah opens her arms to him.

He leans in.

9

Connect with Compassion

> I know I have a true self when my self-protective heart opens up and another person's joy or suffering fills me as if it were my own.
>
> Parker Palmer

I'm at a men's retreat in the Florida Keys when a predawn meditation session goes deeper than I thought possible, and I see three scenes from early in my life.

The first scene feels less like a memory and more like an amalgamation of experiences. In the scene, I'm three, maybe four years old—a soul still becoming accustomed to his body. It begins when I wake up one morning with the enthusiasm of someone who's been given a second chance at life. If every time you go to sleep is a little death and every waking is a resurrection, call me resurrected. I'm eager to try on the magic of existence one more time.

Then, I walk out into the world, run into all the big people, and get really, really confused.

I'm ready to play games—like hide-and-seek—and everyone is definitely playing some kind of hide-and-seek, but no one is cramming themselves into the hamper or pushing themselves to the back of the closet where all the dusty clothes make your nose itch. This hide-and-seek they're playing in plain sight, and it doesn't look very fun at all.

As I watch them play, I can see several things about the game. First, I've been inducted into it. I didn't ask to be a part of it, but the choice wasn't mine. Second, it's a very high-stakes game. There's a lot on the line. Maybe everything. That's why they play it so intensely. Third, the game has many rules I can't understand and only one I can clearly discern: We must never acknowledge we are playing the game.

That sends a chill right through me.

I've been involuntarily thrust into a very important game whose rules I don't know and cannot ask about. It makes me want to do one thing and one thing only. I go back home and into my bedroom, where I can be alone—where I don't have to play the game everyone else is playing.

But sometimes people come into my room.

Scene one fades and scene two takes its place. I think this second scene is a memory, but I can't be sure. I'm not much older, and my favorite books are all open on my bedroom floor. I can't read yet, but my imagination plays with the pictures, and I'm planning to enjoy all my favorite parts right in a row. This preparation has taken most of the day, and I'm just about to start the fun part when my babysitter walks in, announcing the pizza has arrived. She tells me I have to pick up my books before I can eat. My stomach gets queasy like when the car goes fast over that little hill on the way to Grandma and Grandpa's house. Somehow I know this is part of the game. I want to cry, but instead I get defiant. I think I might be playing the game now, too, but I'm not sure.

I go to bed that night without dinner.

Scene two gives way to scene three, several years in the future. This one is definitely a memory. I'm outdoors on a summer night playing laser tag with the neighborhood kids, searching for an unexpected hiding spot from which to snipe my competitors. A family friend is visiting and her car is parked in the driveway. My exuberance doesn't show up as much these days, but tonight I'm like that little boy many years ago, eager to play and assuming we're all going to have fun together. So I ask her if I can hide in the back seat of her car. It's such a simple request it doesn't occur to me she'll say no.

The way she says no suggests there's something very wrong with me for asking.

I'm so taken off guard by it I fail to hide the hurt quickly enough. I'm like a firecracker fizzling at its apex. The light goes instantly out of me. I stumble over my words. Tears spring to my eyes. Everyone can see how easily I was wounded, and that breaks the biggest rule of the game.

In the midst of this memory, our meditation guide invites us to open our eyes to a new day dawning in the Florida Keys. My first thought upon concluding the meditation is, *I know the name of the game*.

It's called Pretend We're Not In Pain.

The Antidote to Disconnection

Your life started exactly the same way my life did, and exactly the same way every human life begins. Someone took a special kind of scissors and cut through the rubbery flesh of an umbilical cord, officially separating you from everyone on the planet. There are no nerve endings in the umbilical cord, so the whole thing was essentially painless. You didn't even know it was happening.

The pain of our human separateness comes a little later.

The first time you're slow to be picked up when you're crying or slow to be fed when you're hungry. The first time something else is more important than you. The first no. The first disappointment in you. The first yell. The first banishment to your room. Sure, loving parents can ease the sting of separation for a while. Some even go overboard in trying to prevent the inevitable, but every human life becomes a lesson in separateness, no matter how well we are loved. Kindergarten happens. Bullies happen. You don't make the team. There's a hundred people in the high school hallway, and you feel invisible to every single one. Bruce Springsteen sings, "I wanna find one face that ain't looking through me."[1] He found millions. He is no less separate.

Separation is the ordinary trauma at the center of every human life.

On a Saturday morning in third grade, I hopped on my bike and pedaled the dusty roads of our trailer park to my only friend's mobile home, where I planned to pick him up for our weekend ride around the neighborhood. When he opened the door to his trailer, I smiled at him as usual, but he didn't smile back. Instead, he asked what I was doing there, as if we'd never met. Behind him, another boy in our class appeared. I'd been traded out for someone else.

And just like that, the pain of separation on a perfectly sunny Saturday.

As an adult, it's easy to forget how painful that was for a little boy. Nowadays, I'd just delete that friend from my contacts, text a dozen other friends, scroll through my social media feed for recent comments, or find some analog connection with my wife and kids. When we were children, though, a moment of separation like that was exquisitely painful, and we have a word for that kind of pain. It's called *loneliness*. Children are basically souls with tennis shoes on. They still know the whole point of existence is to come back together and, in the words of Ram Dass, to walk each other home.[2] So, for a kid, loneliness is *the* fly in the ointment. It's the big problem that must be solved, and it must be solved at any cost.

One of the costs is shame.

As I pedaled back to my trailer on that summer morning, I didn't think I'd been replaced by someone *different*; I thought I'd been replaced by someone *better*. Shame is the belief that we're not good enough—not worthy of love or belonging. However, shame doesn't begin as a belief; it begins as an explanation for our loneliness.

And, believe it or not, it was originally an explanation that *empowered* us.

If the cause of our separateness was outside of us—embedded in the very nature of existence itself—then we could be left behind without notice and blindsided by the loneliness of it over and over again. On the other hand, if the problem was inside of us, then it was a problem we could fix, and therefore we were back in control of the pain. A child would rather feel putrid than powerless in the face of their separation, and thus shame is born into every human life.

I can't remember what I actually did after my friend sent me packing, but I recall very well what I did for the next few decades: I tried to become the kind of person no one would trade out for anyone else. In other words, I played the Pretend We're Not In Pain Game. In this game, we pretend we're not lonely, and then we pretend we're not ashamed of our loneliness. Instead, we strive for attention and awards and accolades, power and possessions and prestige, romance and relationships and reunion. It's an admirable game, and we all have to play it in order to discover that it's also an unwinnable game.

The Pretend We're Not In Pain Game is unwinnable because, ironically, it deprives us of the very thing that can actually connect us.

Now known as Hansen's disease, leprosy was one of those conditions that rocked the ancient world, much like AIDS did at first in our modern world. People with leprosy commonly lost fingers and toes and hands and feet. They walked around with open sores and infections. Sometimes they went blind. Many assumed it was a curse from God, but no one was taking chances about its contagiousness. People with leprosy were shunted off into their own colonies, and their contact with "clean" people was kept to a minimum. For most of those infected, the disease was a gruesome fate.

Enter Dr. Paul Brand in the mid-twentieth century.[3]

Raised in rural India by missionary parents until the age of nine, he was exposed to the stomach-turning impact of leprosy on a regular basis. He then received his education in the United Kingdom and became a doctor like his parents before him. After returning to India to join the staff of a hospital there, he began questioning the assumption that *Mycobacterium leprae*—the bacterium that causes leprosy—directly rots the flesh of its victims. In the course of his research, he visited several villages near a large leprosy hospital in New Guinea and witnessed two scenes that rewarded his skepticism.

A woman was roasting yams over a fire. When one of the yams fell off the stick, she tried to retrieve it by spearing it again, each time pushing the yam even farther into the burning coals. Defeated, she turned to a man nearby, who walked to the fire, reached into the coals, and retrieved the yam. Dr. Brand was horrified and rushed to him. The man had already lost all of his fingers to previous injuries, his wounds were leaking with infections from recent traumas, and his skin was burned badly from this most recent incident. However, he was indifferent to his hand.

A few days later, Dr. Brand was scheduled to conduct a group clinic at a neighboring village. His arrival was announced by the ringing of a bell to summon patients. One young man on crutches began at the back of the crowd but quickly tucked his crutches under his arms and sprinted to the front of the line, smiling proudly with triumph. When Dr. Brand approached him, however, it became clear the man was badly injured. He'd run on a dislocated ankle, putting too much pressure on the end of his leg bone. The skin had broken under the trauma of it, and he was now walking on the end of his tibia. Small twigs and stones were embedded in the bone and the marrow cavity.

The young man smiled on.

The leprosy bacterium, it turns out, does not rot tissue; it kills nerve endings. Without the capacity to feel pain, the leprosy patients lived in ways that wounded their tissues. Then, there was no pain to remind them to tend to those wounds. Finally, they were unconcerned that a part of their body was rotting away because without pain, they felt no sense of connection to that part of their body.

In other words, you think it's your humerus and ulna and radius bones that connect you to your hand. It's not. It's pain that connects you to your hand. Without pain, you wouldn't treat your hand like it's a part of you. And you think it's your femur and your tibia and all the tendons and ligaments running throughout those bones that connect you to your foot. It's not. It's pain that connects you to your foot. Without pain, you wouldn't treat your foot like it's a part of you.

Similarly, we believe we are connected to other people by our presence or attention or words or service or physical affection or thoughts or memories or beliefs or blood or nationality or history or marriage. We're not. While all those things are good and important parts of human relations, the one thing that allows us to care for each other like we are a part of each other—like we're truly connected members of a human body and no longer separate and alone—is our pain. If you cannot feel the pain in another member of the human race, it won't matter how much time you spend with them; you will feel an unsolvable separateness from them. In other words, pretending we're not in pain is like relational leprosy—it robs us of the pain we need to feel in order to be truly connected.

Dr. Brand's discovery changed the way leprosy patients were treated. If they could be diagnosed early enough, before the bacteria permanently damaged the nerve endings, then their sense of pain could be preserved, they'd maintain a sense of connection to their body parts, and they'd be motivated to care for them. Because leprosy is caused by a bacterium, the antidote is a simple antibiotic.

The antidote for relational leprosy is similarly simple. It's called compassion.

Compassion is often misconstrued as a fluffy concept. It can conjure warm images of quiet yoga retreats and hot bubble baths and placid Buddhas and a beatific Jesus surrounded by barnyard animals. That is a domesticated and Westernized kind of compassion. The essence of true compassion can be located in its literal translation from the Latin.

Com, meaning "with." *Pati*, meaning "to suffer." *Compati*, meaning "to suffer with."

In this sense, compassion is quite distinct from pity and even sympathy. Pity creates distance. It feels sorry for the other and wishes their predicament could be another way, but the wish comes from way over here, where we are without such a predicament. Pity is self-containing—the whole act of it is complete in a twinge of regret on someone else's behalf.

Sympathy is softer, but it's not compassion either. Sympathy is sensitivity to someone's pain, along with some subtle relief that we're not all the way in the pain with them. There's a reason they're called sympathy cards and not compassion cards. Thoughts and prayers can be sent, but compassion crosses chasms.

Compassion isn't feeling sorry for a person's story for a while; it's living in a person's story for a moment. Whereas sympathy keeps someone else in your *thoughts*, compassion puts you in someone else's *shoes*, no matter how badly they pinch. Compassion is what happens when you truly join someone in their pain by actually feeling it with them. There's nothing fluffy about that.

Quit Playing the Game

For the rest of the retreat in the Florida Keys, my awareness of the Pretend We're Not In Pain Game deepens. I watch myself play it. I watch the other retreatants play it. The young woman who staffs the coffee shop across the street from the resort plays it. The guy who pilots our fishing boat plays it. The waitress at breakfast on the final morning doesn't seem to be playing it, though I suspect that's because she's playing it so well.

Then I return to Miami International Airport for my flight home.

Usually, at airports I try to avoid people like the plague, in part because I'm concerned they might actually be carrying the plague, but mostly because people at airports are generally miserable creatures. Travelers are openly stressed about their travel, and workers are usually as grumpy as I'd be if I was serving a bunch of stressed-out travelers. The line at Starbucks is always a mile long, and everyone acts the way you'd expect people to act when their next fix has been delayed. At airports—these teeming hubs of interconnection—humans are, ironically, at their most disconnected. On this day, though, I see through it all.

I've quit playing the game.

I see the red rims of the ticketing agent's eyes and feel the tears she must have shed. I wonder who she cried for. The TSA agent who scans my ID is anxiously checking his watch between every traveler, and I feel his anxiety. I wonder what love he's longing to hear from. The woman in front of me at Starbucks looks perfectly calm, except she's picking a cuticle on her right thumb with her forefinger to the point of bleeding, and I imagine the pressure she must feel to look so put together. It's a prison. I wonder which one of a thousand human worries might be troubling her so.

In a word, I feel compassion.

In the original *Matrix* movie, the protagonist Neo played by Keanu Reeves discovers he's living inside a digital simulation run by an AI that has enslaved humanity.[4] The problem is, the simulation is so realistic that when you enter it to overthrow the AI, your death inside the software feels so real that your body actually dies in the material world. During the climactic scene of the movie, Neo becomes an entirely new creature when he sees the agents sent there to kill him not as real agents but as computer code.

It's like that for me now as I walk through the airport. When I see people, I don't see the game we've all been programmed to play since birth—the one we were inducted into without a choice. When I look at the masses of humanity surrounding me, I see past the pretending and into the pain itself, as if it's waterfalling through everyone like source code. Every person I pass is a pain body—a living, breathing amalgam of everything that has hurt them, is hurting them, and will hurt them. In the seeing of their pain, my heart is thrown more widely open than I can ever remember it being. I haven't really spoken to a single one of them, and yet I feel profoundly connected to all of them.

Trappist monk Thomas Merton had his own moment of seeing through the game while standing in a sea of shoppers in downtown Louisville:

> I was suddenly overwhelmed with the realization that I loved all these people, that they were mine and I theirs, that we could not be alien to one another even though we were total strangers. It was like waking from a dream of separateness, of spurious self-isolation in a special world. . . .

> This sense of liberation from an illusory difference was such a relief and such a joy to me that I almost laughed out loud. . . . I have the immense joy of being [human], a member of a race in which God Himself became incarnate. As if the sorrows and stupidities of the human condition could overwhelm me, now that I realize what we all are. And if only everybody could realize this! But it cannot be explained. There is no way of telling people that they are all walking around shining like the sun.[5]

When compassion becomes your default response, connection becomes your default reality.

Stand in Awe

At the beginning of the Peaceful Pivot Process, you couldn't feel your pain; you could only protect it. In the middle of the process, you learned to feel it and to be Okay in the midst of it. Here at the end, you are finally free to feel it in everyone else, too, by embracing the final pivot of the process:

When someone shows you only their protections, you see only their pain.

In my book *Loveable*, I shared a parable told by philosopher and theologian Peter Rollins about Seamus, someone who has retired for good from the Pretend We're Not In Pain Game. It bears repeating:

> A rich Texas oilman . . . discovers he has a long-lost cousin in Ireland named Seamus, whom he then travels to meet. When the oilman arrives, Seamus begins showing his rich cousin around his humble property. After the short tour, the oilman boasts, "You should see my land in Texas. I can't even drive my car to the edges of it." Seamus hears his comparison and recognizes it for what it is—competition, bluster, and self-promotion. And he sees the fractured humanity it is meant to obscure. So, Seamus

looks at his cousin, nods in understanding, and says, "Yeah, my car is broken too."[6]

Compassion is simply the practice of seeing the pain beneath people's protections.

It doesn't take two to do that kind of tango. Seamus didn't need his cousin to open his heart in order to feel compassion for him. It was an inside job. He just opened his heart to his cousin's pain, no reciprocation required. It was a kindness to his cousin, for sure, but it was also a kindness to himself. When your heart is open unconditionally, you are finally free. When your compassion flows freely, you are finally connected. In fact, you can feel deeply connected to a complete stranger—thousands of them, actually, in Miami International Airport—even while they curse at the barista for adding the wrong kind of cold foam, even while they harangue the gate attendant because there are no more seats in first class, even while they look at the crying infant in seat 21D like it's Rosemary's baby.

"Here is what we seek," writes Father Gregory Boyle, "a compassion that can stand in awe at what [others] have to carry rather than stand in judgment at how they carry it."[7]

After I return from the Florida Keys, my heart refuses to close, and it's a good thing, because it's an election year. I see all the levels of self-protection and survivalism layered into our social discourse and I think, "Yeah, my car's broken too." Someone cuts me off in traffic and then waves their middle finger at me. "Yeah, my car's broken too." A vendor tries to rip me off. "Yeah, my car's broken too."

It happens over and over again with strangers and friends and my kids and my wife, and my heart is kept open with a single phrase: *Yeah, my car's broken too*.

Then one Sunday night my wife and I are doing a jigsaw puzzle at the kitchen table, dinner cooking on the stove, when our son Quinn walks through the room and says goodbye as he grabs his car keys from the counter.

"Wait, where are you going?" my wife asks, an edge in her voice.

To his girlfriend's house for dinner, he says.

"But it's a school night," she retorts.

"No, it's not," he says matter-of-factly. "We have the day off tomorrow."

"Have you cleaned your room yet?" she asks, as if dropping a royal flush that will win the hand.

"Yeah, you can go check it," he says, now sounding a little quizzical, as if he's wondering what kind of game she's playing here.

The game she's playing is Pretend We're Not In Pain.

We adore Quinn. We don't idealize him—he's not perfect—but we cherish the many good moments and the occasional hard moments with him. We are also keenly aware those moments are dwindling rapidly. In a year or so, he'll be gone at college on a night like this. We can already feel the separation of it happening. It's the twilight of his childhood. The grief of it is palpable. And now on this night he's having dinner elsewhere, so the number of nights left with him is unexpectedly reduced by one. My wife's heart is closing to the pain of it, and it's about to drive an unnecessary wedge between her and Quinn. It's time to quit pretending.

"He's leaving us one little bit at a time," I say to her. "This next year is going to be really wonderful and really hard. Tonight is practice at feeling the hard part."

I watch the hot air go out of her and then condense in her eyes. They swim as much as my own.

"Oh," Quinn says, seeing our emotion, "should I stay for dinner tonight?"

"No, you *have* to go so we can learn how to feel this," I say.

He wraps us in an unusually long hug before he leaves, but it's not our arms that connect us. It's our pain. It's our compassion. It's our suffering with each other.

Compassion doesn't come easily, but once it does, connection comes naturally.

Free yourself from the Pretend We're Not In Pain Game.

Prioritize the pain beneath people's protection.

Make connection your default condition.

Stand in awe.

Exercise: The Quick Compassion Questionnaire

It's been almost two months of joint appointments since Henry leaned into Sarah's arms and she canceled her plans to go antiquing with her mother. I'd expected to see both of them again today, but it's only Henry on my screen. In the past, his solitude has heralded some kind of fallout between them. Right away, though, today feels different. His energy is easy. Those creases between his eyebrows are at rest.

"You look like the bearer of good news," I say.

He smiles widely. "Sarah said she doesn't need to be here today. We're getting plenty of quality time outside of these appointments."

"And no triggered moments this week?" I probe.

"That's the thing. We did have one that might've gotten really ugly in the past, but we came out of it feeling more connected than ever."

"How'd you pull that off?" I ask, in part because I'm curious and in part because I want him to put words to it. **Integrating our wins is just as important as inspecting our wounds.**

"After you gave us the Quick Compassion Questionnaire a couple of weeks ago, I memorized it so I'd be able to use it at my crossroads. And man, did I need it this week."

"Tell me more."

"Okay. So, I walked out of our bedroom on Wednesday morning, and Sarah and Owen were going at it. He woke up with a fever and Sarah was telling him to get back into bed. Meanwhile, I was supposed to be chaperoning his field trip to the arboretum, and he didn't want to miss it, so he was refusing, and I naturally started sourcing some empathy for Owen from my own story."

Sourcing. He still talks like a businessman. No matter how openhearted you become, you are who you are. I'm nodding him along, marveling at how far he's come.

"I mean, I remember what it was like to miss out on big experiences with friends," he says. "It happened all the time when my mom was down and out and my dad was gone. Anyway, I tried to explain this to Sarah, and Owen took it as a sign that I was aligning with him, so he started acting like it was the boys against the girl. Well, Sarah went *off*. Doc, I've never seen her so angry at anyone, let alone Owen. I could feel my heart closing, so I asked myself the questions you gave us to ask when someone else's heart is closing." He holds up his hands and starts ticking them off on his fingers.

"One: How are they closing their heart? Two: What pain is their closed heart protecting? Three: Where might that pain originate in their story? Four: Am I willing to let them have their protection? Five: Am I willing to feel their pain with them?" He pauses there, shaking his head and smiling with wonder.

"And?" I ask, eager now to hear how it turned out.

"And just like that," he snaps his fingers, "my heart was open to her. I didn't even have to answer the questions completely. The asking of them alone was enough to make me remember that anyone who closes like that is in a lot of pain."

"Were you able to answer the questions at all?"

"Sure," he says, "I could see how Owen and I were replicating a painful part of her story. She loved her older brothers and wanted to be around them all the time. But her dad was very traditional, and he always divided the family along gender lines. The boys would go off and have adventures together, and Sarah would be stuck at home with her mom doing domestic things, pretending to enjoy it. And here we were again: The boys leaving her at home to go on an adventure at the arboretum."

"So what did you do?"

"I just went to her and gave her a hug and reassured her I was on her side."

"Did she open back up?"

"Not right away." He shakes his head, marveling again. "But, Doc, that didn't matter. *I* was open, and my openness didn't depend on her openness. I could feel connected to her no matter what. I could love her in her pain even when she was protecting it. It's like I was . . ." he pauses, searching for the word and failing to find it. I offer to help.

"Free?" I suggest.

A childlike smile appears once more on his face.

"Yeah," he says. "That's it. Free. I feel free."

It's Your Power

> Tranquility is contagious, peace is contagious. One only thinks of the contagiousness of illness, but there is the contagion of serenity and joy.
>
> Anaïs Nin

In a way, this book began in the throes of COVID-19.

The New Year's Eve on which I made the resolution that would change my life—*Moment to moment, I will notice my heart closing and try to open it back up*—was eight months into the pandemic. Lockdown restrictions had eased, vaccines had been released, and the end seemed to be in sight, but most of the people we knew were still social distancing. So instead of hosting our annual New Year's Eve party, our family purchased tickets to a virtual Avett Brothers concert, watched it on television, and went to bed well before that long, long year was officially over. In the morning, I woke up to a new year and a new practice: openheartedness.

Unbeknownst to me, I had exchanged one contagion for another.

During the pandemic, government entities—from the federal level down to local school boards—made the decisions about what we could and could not do during the spread of the virus. COVID-19 wasn't in *control*. However, for more than a year, that microscopic organism wielded enormous *power* all around the globe. It influenced an entire species—eight billion of us—to behave in radically different ways. Here at the end of this book, I can finally share with you this distinction, which is so important yet delicate it may have been inconceivable to you at the beginning:

Control and power aren't the same thing.

Control arises from an anxious energy; power arises from a peaceful energy. Control forces and pressures and restricts; power influences and creates and shapes. Control divides people into the controller and the controlled; power unites people into the empowered. Control imprisons people; power sets them free. Control breeds resistance; power breeds participation. Control is fragile and fickle; power is robust and sustainable. **Control is weakness masquerading as strength; power is strength accepting its weakness.**

A closed heart is an attempt to assert control over the present moment and whoever is involved in it. An open heart, on the other hand, has no interest in control, yet it wields tremendous power. It's the power of contagion, and once you can choose to keep your heart open in any moment, it's your power too.

There's a phrase—*dirt-poor*—that some people think is a slur.

For me, it's not a slur, it's my story.

When I lived in the trailer park—and got around in that old Buick Skylark that wouldn't turn left—there was a huge dirt pile at the edge of the community, left over from its original construction. No one had bothered to move it, and I was glad they didn't, because it was the only place for a boy to play. There was no jungle gym to climb. There were no athletic fields to use. There was no town to wander. There was just the dirt pile, and I made the most of it.

Like I said, I was dirt-poor.

When you're climbing out of that kind of poverty, air travel is both a luxury and a flirtation with financial disaster. You've got no resources to rebook a missed flight. If you're late, you're not going anywhere but home. Not to mention, when I was a kid, GPS was the stuff of sci-fi movies. You had to pull an old Rand McNally atlas from underneath the passenger seat and make your best guess at the fastest way to get there, while keeping your fingers crossed that construction and crashes didn't make you miss your flight. Air travel is stressful for everyone, but for the impoverished, it can feel like you're gambling your livelihood.

It was that kind of air travel trauma with which I showed up to the morning after my wedding.

Up to that point in our relationship, I'd been Mr. Calm-Cool-and-Collected. We'd flown together once, and I'd managed to disguise my anxiety the whole trip. However, that time there was nothing at stake. This time our whole honeymoon was on the line. As poor graduate students, we'd chosen the cheapest flight to Jamaica—six o'clock on a Sunday morning. If we made the flight, it would be just us and a few other bleary-eyed newlyweds on the plane. If we missed it, there'd be no rebooking our honeymoon.

We woke up in the darkness before dawn, and my bride's eyes were irritated from the party the night before, so she didn't put in her contacts, rendering her blind as a bat. She was a seasoned world traveler, but she was trusting her brand-new husband to get her to the airport safely. And why wouldn't she? After all, he was Mr. Calm-Cool-and-Collected.

Cue my air travel trauma as I missed the first airport exit.

After taking the next exit, I was still so flustered that I failed to follow the signs for long-term parking, and I missed the turn into the lot. We had to circle the whole airport again. Another delay. My anxiety went to eleven. It was still dark and there wasn't much traffic, so I punched the accelerator and ignored the traffic signals. As I ran a red light, we were almost T-boned by an airport shuttle, which laid on its horn.

My bride wondered aloud if I'd lost my mind.

Eventually we found parking and made our way to the ticketing counter, rolling our brand-new luggage, which was secured by brand-new combination padlocks. As we hoisted our bags onto the scale to be weighed, the agent informed us we'd have to remove the locks. It was about a month after 9/11, and regulations had changed.

I dropped to a knee, rolled the tumbler on the first padlock into place, and . . . nothing. The combination didn't work. I imagined us missing our plane while figuring out how to remove the locks, and it was too much for my nervous system to handle. I reached in my pocket, took out my car key, raised it over my head like a villain wielding a chef's knife in a horror flick, and prepared to slash into our brand-new luggage with it. What would we do with all our clothes once the suitcase was destroyed? I wasn't thinking that far ahead. My bride, God bless her, grabbed my arm and, instead of suggesting divorce, suggested I try all the numbers adjacent to the combination I thought I'd set.

Lo and behold, it worked.

By the time we reached security, we were truly in a rush, and in my frenzy, I forgot my cell phone in the plastic bin. When I got to the gate and realized my mistake, I reversed direction and sprinted toward security. Remember, this was a month after 9/11—people charging at TSA were not handled gently in those days. Before I could reach the phone, I was basically tackled to the ground. After I proved I wasn't a terrorist and recovered the phone, I made the flight with just minutes to spare.

Now fast-forward another twenty years.

It's New Year's Eve, exactly one year after I made the resolution to notice my heart closing from moment to moment. Our family has just returned from a Christmas vacation in Mexico. The trip there was riddled by delays in the United States and trucks with machine guns in Mexico. Getting back into the country was no picnic either. Due to a second wave of the virus, we needed five negative COVID tests and had to navigate a whole lot of bureaucracy to get home.

We've been back for a couple days, and we're setting our family vision for the coming year. When we get to the one intention we all want to practice together throughout the year, my wife says, "Why don't you tell the kids about your openheartedness practice? Maybe they'll want to do it this year too." I tell them some of what I've told you in these pages, and the table gets very quiet. Then my daughter, who is twelve at the time, speaks up, and this is what she says:

"That must be why, every time something went wrong on the way to Mexico and back, I looked at you and felt calm."

A year into the practice, it occurred to me for the first time that openheartedness wasn't just changing me, it was changing the people around me, too, *even when they had no idea I was practicing it*. I thought about how the world had spent much of the last two years concerned about a contagious virus called SARS-CoV-2, but viruses aren't the only contagious things on the planet. Calmness is contagious too. A calm soul calms souls. A soothed nervous system soothes nervous systems.

An open heart opens hearts.

This is a delicate and risky epiphany because, once you realize it, you'll be tempted to use it. For instance, you may be tempted to open your heart *so that* others will open their hearts. This, though, is not truly openheartedness. It's an impersonation of openheartedness for controlling reasons. That's why I couldn't share this with you at the beginning: You may have been tempted to practice openheartedness for the wrong reasons, which isn't openheartedness at all.

Contagious calmness isn't a good *reason* for opening your heart, it's just a powerful *result*.

As our family agreed to practice openheartedness in the year ahead, I thought about lying there in my friend's bunk bed, before headphones, listening to his parents in the living room. I thought about how, for many years, I'd become like those parents in the various "living rooms" of my life. And I thought about how, in the space of a single year, openheartedness had wrought a powerful change on myself, my family, and our household. It was like our whole trip to Mexico was a living room, and my daughter was listening in from her bedroom down the hall, and, instead of feeling confused, she felt calm.

All of life is a living room, and your people are listening.

It doesn't matter if you're a lover or a leader or something in between, the way you show up to your life will ripple outward into the people around you. That's not control, but it is power. You can let your heart close, be dysregulated, and choose conflict. Or you can peacefully pivot—you can keep your heart open, stay calm, and choose connection. If so, the legacy you leave behind will not be a road riddled with relationship ruptures.

It will be the road less triggered.

Discussion Guide

Below are several discussion questions and a call to action for each chapter in this book. The questions are designed to help you reflect on your own or drive a discussion with friends, family, a book club, your church, your organization, your mastermind, or any other group you are a part of. May this guide deepen your understanding of the core principles of the book and support you as you seek to live even more openheartedly.

It's Your Choice

1. The book begins with the suggestion that everyone experiences repetitive patterns of triggered reactions in relationships. Did you agree with this at the beginning of the book? How did your view change as you read?
2. Dr. Kelly jokingly says several times that his wife's approval naturally opens his heart. What experiences are most likely to open your heart? What do you enjoy most about those experiences?
3. Do you have access to your communication tools in some situations but then close your toolbox in others? Was it encouraging or discouraging to hear that adding

more tools may not be helpful if you don't learn to keep your toolbox open?

TAKE ACTION: Consider making Dr. Kelly's New Year's resolution your mantra in the coming days: "Moment to moment, I will notice my heart closing and try to open it back up." At the end of the week, journal for fifteen minutes about what was difficult about this and what was helpful about it.

Part I: Get Calm

Chapter 1: Sense Conflict Coming

1. Has the black box metaphor made you more aware of your first five senses versus your sixth sense, interoception? Where do you sense your closing most vividly between your waist and your temples? Feel free to tune in to your interoception right now and reflect on what you notice!
2. Dr. Kelly writes, "When our hearts close unconsciously, our relationships rupture unnecessarily." Can you think of a time when 80 percent more warning of your closing would have helped? What would you have chosen to do instead?
3. As you were introduced to Henry and Sarah and read about their conflict the morning after a good night, could you relate to how their hearts were closing before either one of them noticed it? When would the Name Your Number exercise be most helpful to you?

TAKE ACTION: The Name Your Number exercise is supported by the See It Sooner Self-Inventory worksheet. Go to TheRoad Resources.com to download the worksheet for free and start putting your interoception to work for you!

Chapter 2: Disrupt Your Defensiveness

1. Dr. Kelly writes, "You don't defeat your defensiveness by doing *away* with it, you defeat your defensiveness by doing *nothing* with it." Is this idea frustrating or freeing to you? How might it change your approach to your triggered moments?
2. Dr. Kelly illustrates our nine most common defenses with a fictional conversation between two friends in which a political difference arises. Did this change how you think about approaching political conversations? If so, how will you handle them differently?
3. Which of the nine defenses was most obvious to you? Which one was the most novel to you? When you look around at the world, which ones do you most commonly see?

TAKE ACTION: The Categorize Your Closing exercise is also supported by a worksheet: the Closed-Hearted Conflict Cycle template. Go to TheRoadResources.com to download the worksheet for free and start watching your defenses instead of wielding them.

Chapter 3: Cultivate Calmness Before Connectedness

1. Dr. Kelly says it's inefficient to regulate your own nervous system by trying to change other people, the past, or things that are out of our control. Has it helped you notice when you're tempted to change others instead of calming yourself? Have you come across any other helpful metaphors or ideas that illustrate a similar principle?
2. Prior to reading this book, what ideas or practices have been most helpful in cultivating inner calm? Do you think the parable about becoming a larger lake will change your approach to calming yourself?

3. Dr. Kelly asks Henry to leave the session so Sarah can focus on regulating herself. What was your reaction to that decision? Did it feel like letting Henry get away with it, or was it a good way for Sarah to focus on self-regulation, or both?

TAKE ACTION: Dr. Kelly led Sarah through the Margin for Terror exercise, and now you can have him lead you through it too. Go to TheRoadResources.com to download the audio file of Dr. Kelly's guided meditation.

Part II: Get Free

Chapter 4: Simplify the Solution

1. One could argue that the pivot from focusing on our people when triggered to focusing on our pain point is the most important and most difficult step in the Peaceful Pivot Process. Is there anything about it you find particularly difficult?
2. It takes a significant pause to adopt a thirty-thousand-foot view of the congruities and incongruities in our reactions across situations. Have you taken the time to do so? If so, what patterns are you noticing in your own reactions?
3. What do you think are some common words to describe people's pain points? Why do you think some of the same words tend to be shared across people?

TAKE ACTION: In the days ahead, when you notice the closing of your heart, consider practicing the two hands technique. Clenched fist: What experience are you clinging to? Stop sign: What experience are you resisting? Open your arms and breathe: What if you allowed the experience to pass through you like a breeze through an open window? Try it physically if you're alone, or mentally if you're with other people.

Chapter 5: Trace Your Triggers Through Time

1. "Your triggers aren't a present you have to fix, they're a past you get to face." What does this mean to you, and how did your perspective on it change as you progressed through the book?
2. What do you see as the biggest difference between the two questions "What's wrong with me?" and "What happened to me?" How do each of these questions affect us differently in the asking and the answering of them?
3. In a midlife crisis, we double down on unsatisfying A-story solutions and ambitions, whereas in a midlife awakening we go searching for a more meaningful B-story. How might this concept from the hero's journey affect the way you think about your goals, values, and vision for your life?

TAKE ACTION: If you are actively in the process of tracing your triggers through time with Dr. Kelly's sentence completion "This wouldn't be so hard if it didn't remind me of . . .," go to TheRoadResources.com to download a quote graphic of this prompt. Print it out and hang it up or add it to your desktop or home screen—wherever it will best remind you to trace your triggers.

Chapter 6: Feel Your Way to Freedom

1. How familiar with the stages of grief were you before? Did Dr. Kelly's application of them help you better understand how we close and open our heart? What did you learn about how we avoid our pain?

2. What part of the sump pump metaphor feels most helpful to you: appreciating how you started in life, recalling how your float switch got stuck, or learning that intense emotions last only ninety seconds? Why is it most helpful?
3. Dr. Kelly describes the benefits of feeling your pain and allowing it to flow: energy, safety, and resiliency. Which of these benefits is the most appealing to you? Does reading about them make it any easier to feel emotional pain? Why or why not?

TAKE ACTION: In the coming days, whenever you notice anxiety or anger rise up within you, ask yourself, "What sadness might this be protecting me from or preventing?" Journal what you notice. This powerful question alone can become a way of lifting your finger off the float switch when you're ready.

Part III: Get Connected

Chapter 7: Set Boundaries Without Battles

1. Dr. Kelly set a boundary with his nephew and refused to play with him. Did you agree or disagree with this decision? Why? Did it sensitize you to any situations in which you try to maintain closeness with others by ignoring your healthy boundaries?
2. How did the Interdependence Intersection framework impact your view of relationships? What is your default relationship style? Have you ever experienced interdependence? What was it like?
3. How does the Yes, And concept affect the way you think about boundary setting? Which of your boundaries would you first express as a want? Does this feel weak or wise to you?

TAKE ACTION: To support your openhearted boundary setting, go to TheRoadResources.com to download the Yes, And Journaling template. Print it out and set aside thirty minutes to do some nondominant hand journaling about an important boundary in your life.

Chapter 8: Stay Curious During Conflict

1. When your heart closes, how would getting curious about it by asking "Why?" like a kid change your mindset about it? What do you see as the key differences between asking why accusatorily versus curiously?
2. Dr. Kelly writes, "Everything that feels like a failure *of* progress is actually a focus *for* progress." How does this free you up to face your imperfections? What makes it most difficult to approach your failures in this way?
3. Dr. Kelly argues that our limiting beliefs are actually our inner child speaking up, so instead of trying to overcome them, we can try to welcome them. Does that feel defeatist to you? Or the opposite: Does that feel hopeful? Why?

TAKE ACTION: When you sense your heart closing, try to open it back up by asking "Why?" with genuine curiosity. Challenge yourself to extend that curiosity to others as well. Let it be a litmus test of how open your heart actually is.

Chapter 9: Connect with Compassion

1. "Separation is the ordinary trauma at the center of every human life." How much does this statement resonate with you? In what ways does it free you up to trace your triggers through time, even if no extraordinary trauma happened to you? Where do you see evidence of this in the world around you?

2. Dr. Kelly suggests that sometimes shame isn't a belief that was put into us but a belief we generate to regain some control over our loneliness. Does this help explain any shame-based beliefs you might have about yourself?
3. What did you think of the contrasting descriptions of pity, sympathy, and compassion? Is it possible to be compassionate—or truly connect with others—without taking the existence of their pain points into account?

TAKE ACTION: Start actively practicing compassion by using the Quick Compassion Questionnaire to see the pain beneath people's protections. Download a PDF of the five questions at TheRoadResources.com.

It's Your Power

1. Dr. Kelly says that openheartedness and calmness are contagious. Do you see any evidence of that in your life or in the lives of the people around you?
2. What was your reaction to the distinction between control and power? Is it tempting to open your heart *so that* other people will open theirs? What can you do to ensure you're opening your heart without the goal of controlling others?
3. Now that you've finished the book and these ideas have begun to influence your life, are there any ways in which you're already witnessing them have an impact on your relationships or your emotional patterns?

TAKE ACTION: Don't make people guess about why you're showing up differently to your life. Choose one person and share your experience of openheartedness with them!

Are you interested in having Dr. Kelly join you on your podcast? Would you like him to keynote an event for your organization or community? Perhaps you'd like to connect with his online community, *The Less Triggered Tribe*, so you can receive free updates, tips, and videos from him? He also takes a handful of new coaching clients every year.

For more information about all of these opportunities, please go to **DrKellyFlanagan.com**.

Acknowledgments

I have never felt less alone than in the writing of this book, and I'm deeply, deeply grateful for those who have walked with me down this particular publishing road.

First, I want to thank my editor, Kelsey Bowen, who believed in this book from the very beginning, gave me the freedom to be who I am in its pages, and yet wisely challenged me to make every single page even better. Superman says kindness is the real punk rock. I say you are.

To my agent, Kathy Helmers, you have been the constant in my writing career, and an author couldn't be blessed with a better constant. To Stephanie Smith, Lauren Cole, Chris Kuhatschek, and the entire team at Revell, your professionalism is second to none—what a gift to be able to trust my work is in your expert hands. To Brandon Judd, Jay Twining, Jeff Mohs, and everyone at Brand Builders Group, your process and your guidance guaranteed there were no holes in this book. To Isla Lake, Carolina Groom, and the rest of the book fulfillment team at Mission Driven Press, you were fabulous at making sure this book was delivered into as many hands as possible. And to Rhonda Jenkins, who is my director of event operations but so much more—you keep me centered, sane, and spiritually growing.

I am indebted to my online community, The Less Triggered Tribe, who met with me on Zoom the third Friday of every month for a year to discuss and dissect every single idea in this book. You all were the wise filter every word ran through—if it couldn't pass through you, it didn't make it into the book. I am no less indebted to the clients who I've been coaching through these ideas on a weekly basis—by showing up fully to the process, you showed me how it works best.

To my friends—those I see once or twice a year at Front Row Dads retreats, those long-distance friends I connect with occasionally, and the local friends I connect with more regularly—every time I get to see you it feels like a family reunion. I especially want to thank Mike Wagner: I knew we'd rock that masterclass together.

To my wife, Kelly—I learned everything in this book on your relational dime. You are the most generous soul that has ever graced the face of the earth. To my children, Aidan, Quinn, and Caitlin, it was witnessing you arrive in the world with your hearts wide open that ultimately inspired me to open mine again. You are the best three things that have ever happened to me.

And last but certainly not least, here's to you, dear reader. Here's to spreading openheartedness together, until the whole planet is infected by it. Here's to the road less triggered and a *world* less triggered.

Notes

It's Your Choice

1. Malcolm Gladwell, *Blink: The Power of Thinking Without Thinking* (Little, Brown, 2005), 29–30.
2. Michael A. Singer, *The Untethered Soul: The Journey Beyond Yourself* (New Harbinger Publications, 2007), 46.
3. Lori Gottlieb, *Maybe You Should Talk to Someone: A Therapist, Her Therapist, and Our Lives Revealed* (Houghton Mifflin, 2019), 62.
4. Singer, *Untethered*, 92.

Chapter 1 Sense Conflict Coming

1. "Top of the Morning," *Bedford Gazette*, December 12, 2013, https://www.bedfordgazette.com/archives/top-of-th-morning/article_5a812c3b-e35b-5cd2-94f8-7773f3f54e15.html.
2. "Wrongful Death Suit Against GM Fast Tracked in U.S. District Court," Pribanic & Pribanic, July 6, 2015, https://pribanic.com/wrongful-death-suit-against-gm-fast-tracked-in-u-s-district-court/.
3. Clifford Atiyeh, "GM Ignition-Switch Review Complete: 124 Fatalities, 274 Injuries," *Car and Driver*, August 3, 2015, https://www.caranddriver.com/news/a15353429/gm-ignition-switch-review-complete-124-fatalities-274-injuries/.
4. Matt Warren and Miriam Frankel, "Interoception: The Inner Sense Driving Your Thoughts," BBC Future, March 23, 2024, https://www.bbc.com/future/article/20240322-interoception-the-mysterious-inner-sense-driving-your-emotions.
5. Warren and Frankel, "Interoception."
6. Lama Rod Owens, *The New Saints: From Broken Hearts to Spiritual Warriors* (Sounds True, 2023), 55.
7. Antoine Bechara et al., "Deciding Advantageously Before Knowing the Advantageous Strategy," *Science* 275, no. 5304 (1997): 1293–95, https://10.1126/science.275.5304.1293.

Chapter 2 Disrupt Your Defensiveness

1. Will Smith and Mark Manson, *Will* (Penguin Press, 2021), 380.
2. Smith and Manson, *Will*, 382.
3. Smith and Manson, *Will*, 393.
4. Walter Bradford Cannon, *The Way of an Investigator: A Scientist's Experiences in Medical Research* (W. W. Norton, 1945), 59–60.
5. Henri J. M. Nouwen, *Out of Solitude: Three Meditations on the Christian Life* (Ave Maria Press, 1974), 40.

Chapter 3 Cultivate Calmness Before Connectedness

1. F. Kathleen Foley, "*Lincoln* Seeks to Set the Facts Straight," *Los Angeles Times*, April 3, 1996, https://www.latimes.com/archives/la-xpm-1996-04-03-ca-54372-story.html.
2. Jon Kabat-Zinn, *Wherever You Go, There You Are: Mindfulness Meditation in Everyday Life* (Hyperion, 1994), 30.
3. Andy Hobson, "Mountain Meditation," Insight Timer, 2025.
4. Bruce D. Perry and Oprah Winfrey, *What Happened to You?: Conversations on Trauma, Resilience, and Healing* (Flatiron Books, 2021), 142, 144.

Chapter 4 Simplify the Solution

1. Shai Danziger et al., "Extraneous Factors in Judicial Decisions," *Proceedings of the National Academy of Sciences of the United States of America* 108, no. 17 (April 11, 2011): 6889–92, https://doi.org/10.1073/pnas.1018033108.
2. M. Scott Peck, *The Road Less Traveled: A New Psychology of Love, Traditional Values, and Spiritual Growth* (Simon & Schuster, 1978), 25.
3. W. H. Auden, "Night Mail," *The Age of Anxiety: A Baroque Eclogue* (Princeton University Press, 2011), 105.

Chapter 5 Trace Your Triggers Through Time

1. Blake Snyder, *Save the Cat!: The Last Book on Screenwriting You'll Ever Need* (Michael Wiese Productions, 2005).
2. *Star Wars: Episode V: The Empire Strikes Back*, directed by Irvin Kershner (Lucasfilm, 1980).
3. Perry and Winfrey, *What Happened*, 25–26.
4. William Faulkner, *Requiem for a Nun* (Vintage Books, 1975), 73.
5. Henri J. M. Nouwen, *The Living Reminder: Service and Prayer in Memory of Jesus Christ* (Seabury Press, 1977), 22.
6. Perry and Winfrey, *What Happened*, 22.

Chapter 6 Feel Your Way to Freedom

1. Elisabeth Kübler-Ross, *On Death and Dying* (Collier Books, 1970).
2. Mark Nepo, *The Book of Awakening: Having the Life You Want by Being Present to the Life You Have* (Conari Press, 2000), 52.

3. Jill Bolte Taylor, *My Stroke of Insight: A Brain Scientist's Personal Journey* (Penguin Books, 2008), 146.

4. Taylor, *Stroke*, 156.

5. Richard Rohr, *The Art of Letting Go: Living the Wisdom of Saint Francis*, narrated by the author (Sounds True, 2010), "The Weeping Mode."

6. Frederick Buechner, *Wishful Thinking: A Theological ABC* (Harper & Row, 1973), 96.

7. Frederick Buechner, *Whistling in the Dark: A Doubter's Dictionary* (Harper & Row, 1988), 117.

8. Etty Hillesum, *An Interrupted Life: The Diaries, 1941–1943 and Letters from Westerbork*, ed. Jan G. Gaarlandt, trans. Arnold J. Pomerans (Henry Holt and Company, 1996), 96.

9. Richard C. Schwartz, *No Bad Parts: Healing Trauma and Restoring Wholeness with the Internal Family Systems Model* (Sounds True, 2021), 70.

10. Óscar Romero, *The Violence of Love*, trans. James R. Brockman (Plough Publishing House, 2000), 289.

Chapter 7 Set Boundaries Without Battles

1. "Ram Dass—Have a Good Journey—Full Lecture," 2 hours, 50 min, 21 sec., posted August 9, 2021, by Baba Ram Dass, YouTube, https://www.youtube.com/watch?v=9I0MhbJoMbY.

2. Kabir, quoted in "Ram Dass—Have a Good Journey—Full Lecture," 2 hours, 50 min, 21 sec., posted August 9, 2021, by Baba Ram Dass, YouTube, https://www.youtube.com/watch?v=9I0MhbJoMbY.

3. "Co-Dependency," Mental Health America, accessed May 31, 2025, https://mhanational.org/resources/co-dependency/.

4. Richard Rohr, *Great Themes of Paul: Life as Participation*, narrated by the author (Franciscan Media, 2010).

5. Susan Scott, *Fierce Conversations: Achieving Success at Work and in Life, One Conversation at a Time* (Berkley Books, 2004), 12.

6. Kelly Leonard and Tom Yorton, *Yes, And: How Improvisation Reverses "No, But" Thinking and Improves Creativity and Collaboration—Lessons from The Second City* (Harper Business, 2015), 63.

7. Dass, "Journey."

8. John Gottman and Julie Schwartz Gottman, *Fight Right: How Successful Couples Turn Conflict into Connection* (Harmony, 2024), 103–6.

Chapter 8 Stay Curious During Conflict

1. John Green, *The Anthropocene Reviewed: Essays on a Human-Centered Planet* (Dutton, 2021), 251.

2. Keridwen Cornelius, "Biosphere 2: The Once Infamous Live-In Terrarium Is Transforming Climate Research," *Scientific American*, October 4, 2021, https://www.scientificamerican.com/article/biosphere-2-the-once-infamous-live-in-terrarium-is-transforming-climate-research/.

3. James Finley, *The Healing Path: A Memoir and an Invitation* (Orbis Books, 2023), 161–62.

Chapter 9 Connect with Compassion

1. “Badlands,” track 1 on Bruce Springsteen, *Darkness on the Edge of Town*, The Record Plant, 1978.

2. Ram Dass, “Ram Dass Quotes,” Ram Dass, accessed May 26, 2025, https://www.ramdass.org/ram-dass-quotes/.

3. Paul Brand and Philip Yancey, *The Gift of Pain: Why We Hurt and What We Can Do About It* (Zondervan, 1997).

4. *The Matrix*, directed by Lana Wachowski and Lilly Wachowski (Warner Bros. Pictures, 1999), DVD.

5. Thomas Merton, *Conjectures of a Guilty Bystander* (Image, 1966), 24.

6. Kelly Flanagan, *Loveable: Embracing What Is Truest About You, So You Can Truly Embrace Your Life* (Zondervan, 2017), 104.

7. Gregory Boyle, *Tattoos on the Heart: The Power of Boundless Compassion* (Free Press, 2010), 67.

DR. KELLY FLANAGAN

is an author, speaker, concierge coach, and clinical psychologist with two decades of expertise in interpersonal relationships. His thought leadership has been featured in *The 5 Love Languages*, *The TODAY Show*, *Reader's Digest*, HuffPost, and *SUCCESS Magazine*. Kelly's two previous nonfiction books, *Loveable* and *True Companions*, debuted as #1 New Releases in Interpersonal Relations, and his national bestselling first novel, *The Unhiding of Elijah Campbell*, has earned multiple literary awards. Kelly's gift for communicating relationship wisdom in humorous and heartfelt ways has made him a sought-after speaker across various industries, from real estate to health care to professional athletic organizations such as the Green Bay Packers. Harnessing decades of research and practice, Kelly's proprietary process will take you and your relationships to a level that traditional communication strategies can't touch. He is married to another clinical psychologist named Kelly, and they have three children—one adulting and two at home in their small town outside of Chicago.

CONNECT WITH KELLY:

DrKellyFlanagan.com

DrKellyFlanagan.Substack.com

@DrKellyFlanagan

A Note from the Publisher

Dear Reader,

Thank you for selecting a Revell book! We're so happy to be part of your life through this work.

Revell's mission is to publish books that offer hope and help for meeting life's challenges, and that bring comfort and inspiration. We know that the right words at the right time can make all the difference; it is our goal with every title to provide just the words you need.

We believe in building lasting relationships with readers, and we'd love to get to know you better. If you have any feedback, questions, or just want to chat about your experience reading this book, please email us directly at publisher@revellbooks.com. Your insights are incredibly important to us, and it would be our pleasure to hear how we can better serve you.

We look forward to hearing from you and having the chance to enhance your experience with Revell Books.

The Publishing Team at Revell Books
A Division of Baker Publishing Group
publisher@revellbooks.com